IN DISCOVERY

To Susan,

Blessings, everyday!

Much love,

Elise

IN DISCOVERY

Thoughts on an Unfolding Life

Elise Seyfried

ISBN: 978-1-4834-9637-5 (sc)
ISBN: 978-1-4834-9636-8 (e)

Lulu Publishing Services rev. date: 1/22/2019

INTRODUCTION

It has been eight years since the publication of my first book of essays, *Unhaling: On God, Grace and a Perfectly Imperfect Life*, and four years since my third book, *Everyday Matters.* While my life circumstances have definitely been changed by a marriage (Sheridan's), the births of two precious grandsons, various college graduations and other leave-takings, world travels and more writing opportunities, I remain (for better or worse) the same Elise. I am still "in discovery," searching for a deeper meaning in my everydays.

Happily, I very often find it. These little epiphanies happen in the most mundane moments, and I try to capture them on paper. Here are the results of my latest small insights. I hope they encourage you to look at your life and discover your own; trust me, they are there.

Thanks as always to my dearest family and friends, who inhabit these pages and inspire me daily. Thanks also to some amazing editors, including Len Lear, Rochelle Melander, Daniel Maurer, Kevin Ferris, and Larry Carlat, for supporting my writing over the years. I am very blessed.

CONTENTS

SEARCHING FOR (BABY) JESUS

If you are expecting a baby during the early fall, and you spy a determined middle-aged woman lurking nearby, fear not! I only want to sign your baby up to play Jesus in our church Christmas pageant. Our church had always used a plastic doll for Baby Jesus, until I took the helm of our Yuletide spectacle 15 years ago. Plastic indeed! Our nativity would be LIVE, right down to the gurgling infant playing our Lord and Savior!

It has since been my annual duty to keep tabs on all the pregnant women in our congregation and community, in hopes of securing the services of their newborns to play the coveted role of the tiny Messiah. These ladies have to deliver between September and November, and I have been VERY disappointed by the poor planning of some of our families. Babies in July? What in the world were they thinking?

This is a very popular gig as you can imagine, with all the glitz and glamour you would expect from a suburban Lutheran church: the baby's name printed in the bulletin! Sometimes spelled correctly! Complimentary swaddling blanket and pacifier! A 20 minute stint lying in a wooden cradle on a stone floor! What newborn could ask for more? It is a great part for young aspiring actors: in the spotlight through the whole show, with no lines to learn and no rehearsals to attend. I only ask that they be suitably dressed: solid color onesies, with no pictures of zoo animals or "clever" sayings on them ("Mommy and Daddy walked to Bethlehem and all I got was this lousy T-shirt.")

Looking back down Memory Lane, I reminisce about our Jesuses gone by. There was the four month old who rocked so hard that she almost tipped over the cradle. There was the five week old who slept through the whole thing, even the unforgettable trombone and xylophone rendition of "We Three Kings." There were the twins (Jesus and a spare; we switched them out when one became fussy). We've had an African American Jesus and several Catholics, when the Lutheran supply ran low. We welcome diversity, as (no joking here) this is the God we worship.

In our version of the Christmas story, B.J. is carried from the back of the church, down the center aisle, up two stone steps, to the cradle. The carrier is the "Head Angel," who is usually a middle schooler. It's a long, perilous journey for the pair, and my heart is always in my throat (especially on those stone steps). We've always been very lucky, and the Holy Infant has made it safely to the manger. When the occasional Head Angel has appeared in church wearing heels, I make her walk barefoot, which when you think about it is more authentic anyway, right?

Well, last year MY son and daughter-in-law DID plan ahead. Peter was born September 23rd, perfect timing. No more stalking Motherhood Maternity, or sending out flyers through the nursery school. I had my own home-grown Son of Man! I found myself being even more protective than usual because he is mine. I briefly thought of running background checks and getting fingerprints for last year's Head Angel, but decided that might be a tad excessive. I did put extra padding in the cradle to make it more comfy, and when he fussed I personally picked him up, even leaving the pulpit in mid-sermon to do so.

This year we have a preemie, the son of a previous Mary (circa 1999). He is a tiny guy, and so I have paired him with an older Head Angel, an experienced babysitter. I anticipate another stressful Christmas Eve, watching them make their way to the altar, but then,

I imagine the first Christmas Eve was too. I picture a cold Middle Eastern night, the pungent smell of animals in a stable. A hay-filled manger. A frightened young mother, giving birth to a very special baby in a far-less-than-ideal setting.

And so our 16th annual Jesus is born again, into a world that badly needs blessing. May we be in a much better place when I cast the Lord for December, 2018. May we sort out the craziness that keeps us from recognizing that we are all family (dysfunctional though we may be). May we look into the eyes of the tiny person representing God, and promise this little one, and all of us, a brighter tomorrow.

In this harrowing, hectic, holy season, God bless us, every one.

IN THE WEE SMALL
HOURS OF THE MORNING

If, perchance, you ever find yourself awake at 5 AM, give me a holler, because I'm up. Why 5:00 in the morning? I do not need to milk the cows. I do not have a paper route. It is too early to go down to church to work. I am usually down there around 7 AM, which is still 1½ hours before the secretary and the preschool teachers arrive. I get a lot done in the peace and quiet, but being there earlier, when it's still dark, in a big building all alone, does not strike me as the world's wisest idea.

Time was, if I was awake at 5 AM, it was because I'd never gone to bed the night before. I recall fondly the Saturday sleep-ins of my teen years and early marriage. We wouldn't put the coffee on until noon at the earliest. With the arrival of the kiddos, our sleep was much more interrupted for sure, but still we'd sleep late every single chance we got.

Now, I do realize that our bodies need less sleep as we age, but this is ridiculous. I literally cannot stay in bed past 6:00 at the latest—even on my day off. On my precious Thursdays, I come to consciousness, glance at the clock radio, register that I do NOT have to get up…then get up anyway. When I first started awakening before the rooster crowed, I would lie abed, willing myself to get another 40 winks. If I did fall back to sleep, my last dream of the night would be a nightmarish doozy, so that was no help. I finally gave up the fight, and now I am always downstairs before sunrise. Meanwhile, Steve has already been up, read a page or two of a boring book, and gone back to sleep in a living room chair. Talk about your fun couples!

I remember years ago subscribing online to something called "Fly Lady." This was the brainchild of a woman who had housecleaning down to a science, and sent out perky, MANY times a day reminders via email: "Have you polished your kitchen sink yet today? How about scrubbing your bathroom tile grout?" She had specific days and times to do things like laundry (hah!), and swore we all could have magazine-worthy homes with mere days of effort per week. This woman was a big believer in using those very early morning hours to do some chores, and I'm sure I could have the shiniest sink in the neighborhood if I put my mind to it. As it is, I stopped subscribing to Fly Lady because it was all much too much for me. Polish my sink! Give me a break!

I could, of course, utilize these extra, golden moments instead for prayer and meditation. And sometimes, I do (and the days that follow this daybreak spiritual practice do tend to be more focused, purposeful and meaningful days). Most mornings, however, I choose to lollygag my way aimlessly through my first hour. I drink way too much coffee, and surf the internet for the latest news headlines (most of which should be sending me straight to my knees, because they are pretty frightening). And so I launch forth into the world, upset and jittery, the polar opposite of a serene church worker.

As I write to you this morning, dawn is just breaking. For a change, I look out the window and marvel at the beauty of the brand-new day. I remember to thank God for my life: my family, my friends, and all of you. The recent losses of a few beloved members of my church family remind me to take nothing for granted, to savor it all. Early as it is, I'm glad to be up today, and I look forward to whatever will be coming down my path in the hours to come. I may never be that "serene church worker," but I can do my best to start my days with joy and gratitude.

However, I would love some company! Pop on over any 5 AM you like! I'll be wide awake!

"HELPING" GOD

Eight years ago I wrote an essay about my tendency to worry. I mentioned worrying about my children: about young Julie traveling alone to Boston to visit Rose, and about Sheridan when he was onstage performing one of his pieces. I noted the oft-quoted verse, Matthew 6:27 ("and can any of you by worrying add one moment to your span of life?") and vowed to take that wise Biblical advice—let go and, as they say, let God.

Well here we are, eight years down the pike. I wish I could report that I have become relaxed, serene even, a whole different woman. But it's a sin to tell a lie. As I hit 60, I am as bad as I ever was in the fretting department. With two grandbabies in the house I try to be very careful not to "parent" them (leaving that job to their actual parents). What I do, though, is hover silently, when Aiden walks down the stairs by himself (possible major tumble!), or eats what I think is too big a bite of food (choking hazard!). My silent hovering fools no one, of course; in fact, it is probably more annoying than if I'd actually said something.

As for my other offspring, I try not to dwell on where they are and what dangerous things they are undoubtedly doing. Maybe it's foreign travel (Julie's solo backpacking adventure through Europe, Evan's current hiking trip through Argentina). Maybe it's domestic excursions (how fast DOES Patrick drive these days? He had quite the lead foot as a young driver! How late WAS Rose on the subway last night? Why won't that girl carry pepper spray?) Whatever! I put it right out of my mind…for a nanosecond. After that, I snap back to attention, on duty once again.

I am an equal-opportunity fretter. I worry about my extended family, my friends, friends of friends, etc. I am very worried about the planet right now, and feel my recycling efforts are not enough to bring us back from the brink. There was a station in the Advent Prayer Center this year that involved tying knots in a piece of yarn to represent your worries ("tied up in knots"). I run the center, so I don't often have a lot of time to just experience it, but if I did, that would probably be my favorite station. How many knots is it possible to tie in one piece of yarn? I would be the one to find out.

I love the idea of us humans being God's "hands and feet" in the world, doing for others, loving them as Jesus does. Though of course God needs no help to work His wonders, it does feel like a kind of holy partnership when we join forces with the Almighty to do good things. I like to think God delights in our efforts.

In the same vein, I have thought of myself as helping God by keeping a watchful eye on everything and everybody…even when (especially when) I encounter situations I either can do nothing about, or are none of my concern. What's the harm in that, right? Someone has to stay awake nights worrying—why not me?

But here's the thing. God doesn't need, or want, my kind of "help" in this regard. My extensive worrying is really a sign that I'm not trusting Him enough. And I definitely do not believe that my stewing helps God, or anyone, one iota.

At age 60, I'm getting really, really tired of worrying. It's starting to take a toll on my health, and for that reason alone I should try and knock it off. I'd love to stick around a few more years at least—and would love to spend those years relaxing a lot more about the things that currently have me tied up in knots.

My resolutions for 2017 are many, as usual, most of them pipe dreams. Attaining world-class physical fitness. Having a perfectly organized house. Writing a New York Times bestseller. But here's a resolution I know I must try and keep: I will look for the beauty and joy and wonder in my life, and concentrate on the positive. I will remind myself that God's arms hold my kids tighter than I ever could. And they hold me as well.

I will probably never have a knot-less piece of yarn at the prayer center, but fewer knots? I think it can happen. Maybe even this year.

PURELY RESEARCH

I do work hard in my office at church.

Promise.

But you'd never know it to look at my browsing history on my computer.

Why, just the other day, after checking the weather (more spring snow predicted for Philly!!! Panic time!!!) and the news headlines (too depressing to recount), I checked out the following:

* Kate Middleton's new maternity coat (just because)
* Top 10 things to do in Lombok (Evan is trekking around the world. He just finished a hike through the Borneo jungles and is headed for the beach in Lombok, Indonesia. I'm all primed if he needs advice on which temples to visit.)
* Secret to Cleaning Gunky Kitchen Cabinets! (Mix vegetable oil and baking soda and apply! Must try!)
* Fifth Ave. Apartment Sold for Record $77.5 million (and here my two Brooklyn based daughters are always looking for cool places to live! They just missed out!)
* Rachael Ray's Spicy Lamb Sliders with Harissa (dinner this week. Extra Google search for what the heck harissa is).
* Holy Week, The Cross, and Children (ah! At last! A web article that relates to my job!)

* 9 Ways to Make a Good Living as a Writer (aaand I'm off track again!)
* Waxed Paper Stained Glass Butterfly Craft (for church! For church! Back to it!)
* Kris Jenner, Momzilla (not exactly a Woman of the Bible, so…)

And so on. The World Wide Web is both paradise and pitfall for an ADHD sufferer like me. I never would have taken the time to go to the library and look all this stuff up, when I was young, so I got a lot of actual work done in school. I would probably have been a straight D student now (unless I could do a senior project on "Kris Jenner, Momzilla"). I grew up in the Dark Ages, prior even to dial-up. Remember dial-up? That strangled duck sound as we got connected? It was a nuisance, because we couldn't use our phones and be online at the same time (believe it or not, kids!). But now it's all easy, too easy.

I try to only peek a couple of times per day, instead of clicking on one site after another, ad infinitum. But, invariably, one view whets my appetite for more, and suddenly an hour has passed and I'm still rating Lombok temples. And Evan hasn't even asked me to do so!

I like to think I'm a good researcher, thoroughly investigating all sources when a topic piques my interest. It's a shame that most of my interest-piquing topics have very little relevance to my daily life (when will I have a need to describe Kate Middleton's maternity wear?). And the more I'm procrastinating about things I actually need to get done, the more fascinating my little detours become.

It's worse now that I have an iPhone. I can waste my time even when I'm NOT at my laptop, looking up this and that random thing. And it seems the rest of my family are no slouches in this department either. At the dinner table, it's a race to see who can whip out their phone fastest to name all of Meryl Streep's Oscar nominations, to discover the winners of the 2005 World Series. We used to rely on our brains to recall these facts. No need now! As long as there's wi-fi we can know it all in a trice!

The Pandora's box that is the internet has been opened, and there's no going back. No more bookshelves laden with dusty, dated volumes of Encyclopedia Britannica for me. The world of knowledge is at my fingertips 24/7. So I need some more self-discipline. The next time someone asks me the name of Stephen King's first book, or even for directions to the mall, I will actually stop and think about it. And I will probably answer wrong, but at least I'll have tried to figure it out on my own.

Meanwhile, let me just check out the guy who sued Pizza Hut when he broke his tooth on a crouton. Then I'll get right to work.

Promise.

BOWLED OVER

I can't tell you how excited I am about the Super Bowl Sunday!! Really, I can't. Because I'm not. Oh, I'll probably wander through the family room at ad times, just to see what edgy humor and special effects a jillion bucks a minute buys these days. I might catch a glimpse of the halftime show, because I've been a fan of Justin Timberlake's since I was a little girl. But the gridiron competition itself? Not at all.

For one thing, I lack the background info necessary to truly appreciate the game: which teams are playing, for example. How the game is actually played, for another. Only one of our kids played football in school. Patrick was a place kicker. I faithfully attended the Upper Dublin High School games. However, after he kicked, I always tuned out the rest of the game, and therefore can't tell my fullbacks from my halfbacks from my 3/8 backs.

But more importantly, I lack the interest. And at this point in my life, I'm not afraid to say it. I have learned that the sky will not fall if I am not keen on this or that subject. But it wasn't always this way.

I used to be an utter fraud. Because my husband Steve was a rabid sports fan, and because I was a rabid Steve fan, I feigned wild enthusiasm for the World Series, the NCAA Final Four Tournament, and the PGA tour. Couldn't wait to get up early and catch the action at Wimbledon. Never mind that, deep down, I would only have been intrigued by tennis if McEnroe and Connors were lobbing, say, a live ferret back and forth over the net.

For the first few years we were together, we hosted a small Super Bowl party. Actress that I was, I rooted for the star quarterback as he snaked through a line of behemoths en route to that silly little victory dance. On pain of death, I'd still be unable to recall a single team or player from those golden days of sport. Can't even remember the commercials. Just a total blank.

By the way, my make-believe enjoyment extended to the Bob Dylan tickets I bought for us in our dating days. What, I ask you, is the big deal about Dylan? Steve thinks he's wonderful. I do not get it. But I was there, and dutifully rose to my feet with the crowd while The Great One mumbled that the times they were a changin'.

Around about year four of wedded life, I finally dropped the facade. Miraculously, my marriage has survived the following revelations: 1) I truly detest Bob Dylan songs. 2) I will NEVER carry Steve's golf clubs again. I'd once done this for 18 very painful holes at the Valdosta (GA) Country Club, in my quest to be a stellar girlfriend. 3) The second my hubby leaves the room, I switch from Sports Center to the Food Network. 4) I hate the Olympics! It seems they come along every three months or so, hyped to the nth degree. I am afraid to watch the young athletes' dreams crash and burn when they slip doing a triple axel, or bungle it on the balance beam; I am convinced that I am a jinx, and feel they have a better shot at success if I stay far, far away.

So what are my plans for Sunday evening?

Nothing involving touchdowns, that's for sure. The Crown Jewel of American Sports will glitter on without me. That leaves some popcorn in the bowl, and an open spot on our sofa. If you're a fan, come on by. You and Steve can cheer yourselves hoarse. I am, officially, bowled over.

SHELL GAME

A lot (let's be honest, most) of nature, I could take or leave alone. In my heart, I remain a girl from New York City, a decidedly un-natural place. Majestic rock formations? Towering sequoia trees? Ho hum! But time was, if you showed me a seashell, for some reason I was all over it. Big, small, occupied, unoccupied, broken, intact—didn't matter! I loved them all!

Growing up, summertime meant weeks at the Jersey shore. Every year, my first stop was the Bait and Tackle Shop in Normandy Beach, which, in addition to their signature fishing supplies, also sold exotic seashells. Those bivalves and mollusks were my primary seasonal purchases. For hours on end, I pored over my *Guide to the Seashells of the World.* By age seven, I could tell you (much) more than you wanted to know about the giant tridacna clam, the rarest types of cowries, and the poisonous creature housed in the cone shell. I day-dreamed about discovering colorful marvels of the sea in Indonesia and Madagascar, in Sanibel, Florida and on Padre Island, Texas.

Alas, the shells I actually found on the beach in my New Jersey collection consisted mostly of broken clams (the infrequent whole shells I would give to my Aunt Rose, who used them as "ash receivers" for her cigarettes) and smelly dead mussels tangled up in seaweed. But I was not deterred. Someday I would travel far and wide seeking treasures from the deep!

After my husband Steve and I founded the Rehoboth Summer Children's Theatre in 1982, I spent every July and August walking the Delaware beaches, and had a bit more luck. The ocean surf wasn't quite as rough as in New Jersey, and the Delaware Bay was quite calm, so more shells survived the trip to land in one piece. My enjoyment of this hobby increased a thousand fold after my children came along. All five kids loved shell hunting at the beach and, like their mother before them, loved spending their allowances at the Sea Shell Shop on cameo shells and chambered nautiluses (nautili?).

Once in a while, there would be a special find. I recall my elation the day a strange tide suddenly dumped huge quantities of starfish on the sand. Of course, I had no idea what to DO with these live creatures after I filled a bucket with them. While I was figuring it out, I left the bucket outside behind our cottage. Within an hour, the many stray cats in town had made my decision for me: they found the starfish and tore them all apart.

My vacations in Jamaica and Hawaii, and mission trips to Costa Rica, yielded some beautiful specimens, but I've noticed that my collecting has slowed down markedly in recent years. My other interests have eclipsed this one, and as I hit age 60, collections in general have lost their luster. They seem to be just more "things" in a life already chock-full of them. Now I can stroll for hours along the shoreline and not pick up a single shell. I pass by the perfect snails and oysters, and tell myself I am giving a gift to little shell-seekers who will soon follow my path. Sometimes my change of attitude makes me sad—it's as if my shell-mania was a last connection to the wonder of my childhood, and now it's finally over.

But I'm not quite ready to pitch the shells I still possess. There is a bowl of scallop shells on my desk at work, and a huge basket of conch shells in the family room at home. I may never again pick up another seashell myself, but maybe, as long as I keep what I have, that long-ago little girl, and the thrill of her discoveries, will remain with me somewhere down deep. And maybe that is something worth holding on to after all.

BE MINE?

Happy almost Valentine's Day, everyone! How did last February 14th go for you all? Candlelit dinners in fancy restaurants? Massages at the spa? Diamond bracelets? Good for you! My sweetheart of a husband Steve has never pulled off a big Valentine's Day treat for me (he treats me just fine all year long), but that's OK. My expectations for this rather silly holiday are pretty low.

When I was little and in Catholic school, my mom always forgot to buy those Valentines that came 30 to a box, with Daffy Duck and hearts on them, until the very last minute. As a result, we only had time to scribble a message on a few. But that was not a problem, because giving them out in class was very hit-or-miss. My teacher, Sister Vincent, couldn't have cared less about our tender feelings when some of us only got one or two, and others a brimming book bag full. I used to wish the cute kid who always brought great smelling, garlicky sandwiches for lunch would give me a Valentine. But nope! I got them from a boy who tried to impress me once by eating an entire box of Crayolas (he promptly threw up in "eight brilliant colors").

By the time my kids came along, children's tender feelings ruled the day. The expectation in elementary school was clear: everybody had to get Valentines from everybody, or no one would get Valentines from anybody. This fair-handed approach to romance was a bonanza for Hallmark, but a pain for parents. Every year, just as my mother had, I bumped into other moms in the store on February 13th, frantically scooping up 30 to a box cards (still, amazingly, with Daffy Duck and hearts on them) then rushing home to "help" our first graders write out their classmates' names (a painful procedure indeed). Some overachieving parents always upped the ante by attaching lollipops or little bags of M&Ms to THEIR Valentines, while the rest of us just sent in smudged and crossed out wishes for the whole class.

When our brood was in high school, long stemmed roses and candy grams were delivered to classrooms (National Honor Society fundraiser or some such). Being a couple was a BIG DEAL come mid-February…and not being a couple was, alas, a bigger deal. So much for sparing tender feelings! At the age when self-esteem was at its shakiest, the popular/unpopular line was clearly drawn, thanks to savvy marketers of seasonal chocolates and flowers.

I do have to say my children's handmade cards to me over the years were pretty cute. They would be left on my pillow, which would be anointed with Elmer's glue dripping off the red construction paper. Unlike the manufactured kind (Daffy Duck, anyone?) I have kept many of these gems. They were especially flowery when penned by a child who was currently in trouble for some misdeed. How can you put a kid in timeout when she has just written "I adoar you Mom?" One of my favorite Valentines, from Patrick, was signed, "Love, PJ Seyfried," just in case I was wondering who in the world "PJ" was.

As I was married very young, I got to skip the "dateless on Valentine's Day" ordeal, but I know plenty of people, male and female, who suffered through years of this nonsense. One friend, I swear, had a string of beaux who all conveniently (for them) broke up with her in late January. Isn't life tough enough without having other people's joy thrown in your face for an entire 24-hour period of time every year? And as a restaurant worker many years ago, I dreaded the onslaught of teenage Valentine's daters (almost, but not quite, as much as the New Year's Eve revelers). Many young couples, all decked out, would arrive at our upscale eatery, and attempt to order alcohol, flashing their fake IDs (to no avail). They'd select the cheapest thing on the menu, then pay in cash to the dime (meaning, no tip). How adorable!

Lest I sound like The Valentine Grinch, I do applaud any and all efforts to spread a little love in this crazy mixed up world. I would just like to step back a bit from the commercialization frenzy, and see us offer simple, sincere, inexpensive and inclusive sentiments to one another—and not just on February 14th either, but every day.

Meanwhile, Happy Holiday named for a third century Christian Martyr! I only ask that you lucky recipients keep your diamond bracelets to yourselves. The rest of us don't want to know.

IF YOU GIVE A MOUSE A HOUSE

This morning, it was unmistakable. As I came downstairs and walked through the living room, the rustling sound coming from the pile of wood beside the fireplace told me: it's still here. Our latest mouse, I mean. Steve made a valiant effort to catch it, but as he moved the wood, our tiny friend skedaddled across the room and under the sofa. We are having company tonight, and I can only hope little Mickey (or Minnie) makes him (or her) self scarce during dinner. But there's no guarantee, alas. At any moment this evening we may be treated to a flash of fur zooming from here to there. If our guests are reading this, apologies in advance!

Not sure what we're doing wrong. We've set multiple traps all over the house, filled with a gourmet extravaganza—cheese, peanut butter, chocolate. While once in a while the traps are sprung, often both goodies and mousie have disappeared by the time we check. Mind you, in the past we've only had these pesky visitors a few times a year, so it was no big deal—until recently, when the word apparently got out that our home was a perfect Mouse B&BLD (bed and breakfast, lunch and dinner). We called an exterminator, who found their hiding spots and sealed up places they've been using for entrance from outdoors. That seemed to do the trick, for a while. But we once again have been invaded by at least one mouse, and I fear it is not alone.

Our neighbors also have mouse challenges; I know it's not just us. But I am a bit amused at the evolution of my attitude since childhood. Back in the day, one of my favorite books was *Stuart Little*, E.B. White's classic about a dapper mouse in search of his bird friend Margalo. Of course, the Disney mice were adorable, if a little weird, with their human clothes and voices. I never had a pet mouse, but knew kids who did, and I thought they were precious. Now, as a New York City girl I well knew the difference between mouse and rat. The latter always terrified me when I'd spy the occasional one in an alley or by a garbage can—and for good reason: city rats are large, filthy disease carriers. But at some point, I transferred my terror to the harmless, miniscule field mouse, and I became the cliché: leaping onto a chair when I'd see one.

Truth be told, I harbor an intense dislike of squirrels as well. I know, I know—but what are they, after all, but rats with fluffy tails? Years ago, our attic was invaded by a squirrel. She (he?) greeted me one day as I climbed the attic stairs with a bag of my winter clothes. That was bad enough, but she had a mouthful of my kids' school papers and drawings. Seems she was trying to build a nest out of Evan's third grade book reports, and from the looks of things she was making progress. I fled down the steps in horror, but soon resolved to deliver Suzy Squirrel her eviction notice in the form of a Hav-a-Heart trap.

Later, after Steve deposited Suzy in Fort Washington State Park, I read that squirrels have been known to find a place they've been before, up to five miles away. It dawned on me: the park is only THREE miles from our house! Ever since, we've been on the lookout for our uninvited guest. So far so good, though there is a strangely familiar looking rodent I've locked eyes with a few times on my morning walk. It's silly to believe Suzy has found us again, isn't it? Isn't it?

Getting back to the little fur ball in the living room this morning, I know things could be much worse: giant roaches, scorpions, carpenter ants. We humans sometimes have to share our living spaces with a wide variety of unwelcome pests, and if I had to choose a plague on my house, I guess I'd prefer mice to other yucky alternatives. So tonight, I will read grandson Aiden *If You Give a Mouse a Cookie* before he goes to bed, and remind myself that all God's critters, indeed, even our resident varmint, have a place in the choir.

RESOLUTE

Just have a feeling. 2016 is gonna be my year. I stopped making New Year's resolutions quite a while ago when it became clear that, however many times I put them on the list, I was not actually <u>ever</u> going to learn to speak Italian, play chess, or parallel park. My pantry remains a jumble of boxes and jars and cans arranged without rhyme or reason. My windows remain unwashed and my floors unwaxed. My computer files are organized like a treasure hunt, with "work" folders containing recipes and "home" folders filled with Sunday School lesson plans.

On a more personal level, I still have to have the last word in any argument with my husband Steve, I still interrupt entirely too much, I continue to nag the kids. It seems I am, as 2016 dawns, exactly as incompetent and imperfect as I was in 1976. So why should this year be any different? Because THIS year, I have an ingenious plan! I will set the bar lower—a good bit lower. 2016 won't see me clipping coupons and feeding the family for a pittance. It will, however, be the year I will save a whole dime per week by buying the house brand of yogurt at the store instead of the Dannon's (by next December I can treat the gang to $5.20 worth of fun). I may not—ever—win any Good Housekeeping prize, but I will remember to clean out the lint filter in the dryer, at least once in a while, and haul out the vacuum cleaner at least bi-monthly (not to say I will vacuum, but I will haul it out so it makes it seem as if I did).

In the health and fitness department, I won't put "start running again" down in ink anywhere, but I will happily vow to "walk from the house to the car on a regular basis." I will use my paid-up yoga classes…to give as gifts to friends who actually practice yoga. I will dust off my Jane Fonda workout videos from the '80s. Mind you, I will not actually move off the sofa, but just watching the silly workout clothes and big hair of the filmed participants will give me a good belly laugh—and after all, don't they say laughter is the best medicine?

In the relationship arena, I will add "and many more" to all my future Facebook birthday greetings. I will make every effort to call my sister Carolyn in Hawaii when it is NOT 3 AM her time. Why is the six hour time difference so darned hard to remember? In any event, why does she always have to be so crabby when she picks up the phone? When I send a very personal email to a friend in need, I will try not to accidentally cc my entire list of contacts.

In my dealings with my husband and children, I will only have the last word in my arguments when I'm right. I will only interrupt if what I have to say is more important. I will only nag the kids when they aren't doing something they should be doing, or when doing something they shouldn't. This plan is guaranteed to improve my behavior by at least 1-2%! At this rate, 100% improvement is a mere 50-100 years away!

I will also pad the list with things I will, reliably, NOT do. This year, I vow not to play, or watch, pro football. Not to vacation on Fiji. Not to skydive or jet ski or go spelunking. I promise I will not win an Academy Award, or a Nobel, or the lottery. No counted cross-stitch for me, or preserving the bounty from my garden (canned gout weed, anyone?). No checking the oil in the car (after 43 years as a driver, I couldn't begin to tell you how to even do that).

It's shaping up to be a great and extremely doable list. I anticipate success upon success. When I toast 2017, I'll be able to look back with pride on the year when I kept every single one of my New Year's resolutions.

And how many people can say that?

WALKING FISH

I'm sure you've heard the phrase "like a fish out of water" to describe people out of their environment, out of their comfort zone, out of their depth. Well, that was Steve and me for two weeks last month in Spain and France: we were two fish, definitely out of water.

We (well, let's be honest—I) approached this whole adventure with much trepidation. We tried to pack clothes that would make us appear more like locals (albeit locals who stash their cash in hidden bags and belts) than tourists. We speak one language, with small, not particularly helpful, smatterings of a few others. While my memorized "una cerveza, por favor" did indeed get me a beer, my sole other Spanish (a nonsense song about the months of the year I learned in first grade) did us no good whatsoever. In Paris, I could order dinner just fine, but otherwise? My brain helpfully recalled stretches of Stendhal's novel *Le Rouge et Le Noir* which we had to read in Madame Kohn's French 4 class. I can assure you, it's not a great conversation starter in the City of Lights. We are also very unused to long international flights, foreign transit systems (the Lansdale-Doylestown SEPTA line is about our speed), and the ubiquitous euro.

What we don't know about being cosmopolitan Europeans could fill a book (and did—I kept a journal). At first, it didn't even seem like we were cosmopolitan Americans. We had a heck of a time just figuring out the subway from Penn Station in New York to JFK. From trying vainly to scan our passports at the airport's self-serve kiosks to repeatedly inserting our Metro cards upside down, it was starting out as a National Lampoon Vacation (right down to the "funny" scene where we accidentally knocked over the rope delineating the queue for security).

Once we landed, the Seyfried Follies continued. We got turned around countless times on Barcelona's narrow, winding streets, as well as Paris' wide boulevards, despite guidebooks, maps and iPhone apps. We tipped when we didn't need to (it's almost always included in the bill) and didn't when we probably should have. We ordered Café Americano every morning expecting—well, American coffee, and instead got teensy cups of watered down espresso (I took to ordering two cups at a time just for me, and still felt under-caffeinated). There were moments, as we were clearly, and purposefully, striding in the opposite direction from our intended destination (indecision would make us targets for theft, we had heard), when I wondered just why we thought we could handle a trip like this.

But as the days went on, we began to feel a bit more comfortable. Evan's presence in Barcelona (he is living there this year and studying for his Master's degree) helped hugely. Not only did Evan have a great place for us to stay, but he was really knowledgeable about the nuts and bolts of transportation, the must-see sights, the best tapas bars. The other huge help? The warmth and kindness of the people (yes, even the Parisians!). No one laughed at our pronunciation of "gracias" or "s'il vous plâit." We were served fabulous food and drink with genuine smiles; patient passersby gave us directions to this museum or that cathedral. Though we'd been warned about pickpockets, we emerged with all possessions intact (and frankly never saw any suspicious behavior). While the street signs were sometimes missing or hard to see (not unlike, ahem, Philadelphia), I have to say both cities were pretty darned user-friendly—or maybe we just became better "users" over time.

I recently read about a species of fish that live in Thailand known as walking fish, who have developed the ability to spend large amounts of time on land (they can even climb rocks!). They have somehow biologically adapted, to allow them to survive and thrive. So maybe, just maybe, Steve and I might have been "walking fish" as well: out of water, perhaps, but gradually learning to successfully navigate a completely different—and wonderful— environment. Climbing to new heights of experience and understanding. So very thankful for this chance to see another part of our amazing world.

CART BEFORE THE HORSE

I am always getting ahead of myself. I am often guilty of speaking well in advance of a thought process. For this I blame my upbringing. My mom and sisters were so chatty that I would jump in and say whatever, just as a placeholder. This fine tradition continues in my house to this day, with five kids and now grandson Aiden all jockeying for talking privileges. At age 60, I am prone to leap to the head of the conversation queue and then, when I have everyone's attention, promptly forget whatever it was I was going to say. Not to waste my "turn," I blab instead about something totally random.

In school, I worked my way backwards from writing the conclusion of my term papers. As you can imagine, this method could cause significant problems...the boffo ending sometimes bore little relation to the eventual theme of the essay (but I kept it anyway). Nowadays my trick is writing titles for my pieces long before I have a clue about content. This is true for my blog posts, my church newsletter articles, but most of all my children's messages. The second I look at Sunday's lessons I run with the first title that leaps into my head, and later have to write something that more or less goes along with my catchy little word or phrase.

In other areas of my life, I've been known to plunge headlong into an acquaintance (even a courtship), without a clear idea of where the relationship is going. Instead of letting the other person lead the way, ever, I attempt to grab the steering wheel, trying to skip right to the destination (I just met my new best friend!!! This stranger will be my spouse!!!) without taking the slow but necessary steps to get there.

This is, as my Grandma would say, putting the cart before the horse. As we all know, the horse should really come first—at least if you want to get anywhere. But there I am, stubbornly placing my cart right in the horse's way, blocking off what could be wonderful possible avenues ahead.

In matters of faith, it is so easy to do this: to try and call all the shots, even when we don't have a clue about what is ahead. To hastily write a title for our life story, and then scramble to make it fit, without seeking any input from God. And then we are disappointed and frustrated when our reality doesn't match up to what we had rashly decided would, or should, happen. Instead of putting God in God's proper place (the driver's seat), we plant our "cart" (our emotions, our hasty judgements) right in the way, and then wonder why we aren't getting anywhere.

What would our lives be like if we truly trusted God's plan for us? If we stopped second-guessing? If our prayers consisted more of listening, and less of talking about what WE want to do, what WE want to have happen (I'm saying this about myself)? We control freaks don't handle mystery well at all…give us a neat and tidy (and speedy) wrap-up every time! But life is filled with mystery, whether we like it or not, and God's ways can indeed be unknowable to us. But maybe, since we don't exactly have the mind of God, that's OK.

Except for my visits to Amish country, I've never ridden in a horse and buggy, but I "get" the horse and cart analogy. By putting the horse first, to lead us, the journey is possible—even wonderful. So may I get out of God's way and resume the journey of life, following my Lord and trusting in my safe passage on the road, and my Heavenly destination at the end. I believe that someday, the ups and downs and detours will all make sense. For now, I will try to stop getting ahead of myself. Working closely with my divine Co-Author, I will start trusting that the right title will come in due time, after my story is written.

THE ADVENTURES OF CAPTAIN S.

Been doing this for 16 years now—Vacation Bible School, that is. The theme may vary (Galactic Blast! Shake it Up Café! Hero Central!) but the basic setup is the same: 50 some odd 4-8 year olds descend on church for a week of fun, frolic and only occasional injury (we outlawed piggyback rides after a nasty spill in 2012, and since then have faced nothing more dire than scraped knees). We always have VBS in late June, which is ridiculous because it is always immediately before the high school mission trip, but the way I see it—in two weeks, it's ALL over, and then I can enjoy the rest of summer. Getting through those two weeks, though, can be a tad overwhelming.

As "Captain S" (this year we are on a VBS Rolling River Rampage, and I apparently lead groups of rafters through whitewater rapids), my primary job is to enthuse, loudly. "Good morning kids!!" I shriek with supposed delight. "Who's ready for Adventure on the River??" Well, they ALL are of course (except for little Susie who is also shrieking—for her mama). I lead the opening assembly time, 30 minutes of hyperactivity during which I chat with the puppet of the year (this time a purple river otter named Romper), teach the week's Bible verse and "rapid reminders" for each day "Find Joy (Peace, Rest, etc.) on the River!!" and show a short video. Usually I have a music leader who is in charge of introducing the six songs the kids will learn (with motions) before the production for the parents on Friday.

This year, we had to move the date of VBS a week later because of delayed school closings. As a result, my go-to music leader, Sheridan, leaves with Yaj and the kids for Taiwan tomorrow. Other idle musical types are in short supply, so I foolishly decided to tackle the role myself. We just finished Day One and introduced three songs. I recall the cringe-worthy days of my long ago theatre auditions ("actors who can dance"). I was always the one who turned left when the others turned right, or failed to turn at all. We are using a music video for the first two days (Sher never needed this crutch) but as of Wednesday the little ones will have only me to copy. I picture the final performance as a danse macabre, with my tiny troupe lurching confusedly from motion to motion, all out of sync with the music.

But this too shall pass, and the soundtrack of my days will switch abruptly from Kidz Bop to Contemporary Christian hits as we sing during our evening gatherings at our Houston mission trip site. Will I remember that my charges are older teens, not four year olds? Will I be reminding them to go to the potty, eat their snack, take turns with the ball? We will be doing construction work, a far cry from the gentle crafts of this week. Will I be able to transition from playing with modeling clay to hanging drywall?

As usual, I neglect to rely on God to get me through—and, as usual, God gets me through anyway. VBS will no doubt go well, despite my (literal) missteps, as will the mission trip. Two weeks from now, I will look back and marvel: it all happened.

At age 61, I do sometimes look back and marvel in general. I made it to this moment. 16 Vacation Bible Schools and mission trips and untold other ups and downs…all the precious stuff of life. So I will muddle as best I can through the haphazard choreography this week, and the house painting and insulation installing next. And I will give thanks for the rich variety of existence, and look forward to the next challenges and joys.

But first, if you'll excuse me, I need to practice our VBS theme song AGAIN. Arms up? Arms outstretched? And what about our feet?

Wish me luck!

REALITY, VIRTUALLY

Rose's first project as a producer premiered in May at the Tribeca Film Festival in NYC. "Broken Night" was also shown at the Cannes Film Festival in France, and just this week won Best Virtual Reality at The One Club's One Screen Awards. This has been exciting for her, as it is not just an ordinary short movie. This is an interactive "virtual reality" experience. VR has already been used in video games, but using it in film is relatively new.

The viewer puts on a headset, through which the movie is seen. Throughout, said viewer makes choices that determine how the plot will play out. This sophisticated setup actually tracks your vision, and adapts depending on which character you are looking at at a given time. I believe everything ends up in the same place, but it's the getting there that changes from person to person. As you can imagine, this involved filming different scenarios for each choice made, so it was quite the production.

"Broken Night" stars British actress Emily Mortimer in the leading role. The storyline revolves around an unstable woman's undependable memories of a crime—a shooting in her home following an argument with her husband. An intruder is involved. Did she pull the trigger? Who was shot? A detective stands in for the viewer, asking questions, trying to clarify the sequence of events.

I haven't yet seen the film, but I sense it has the quality of a dream, where our self-conceived plots take weird twists and turns that we orchestrate subconsciously. Within our dreamscape, every-thing feels real—but there are certain moments when we are aware that it is NOT real. My reality check often comes when I am in peril. The thought surfaces: this is not happening. I awaken, and wonder about the strange choices my mind made in the dead of night, to steer my story one way or another.

In a way, VR imitates our "real" lives, as we make the daily choices that affect our outcomes. Like VR, we may interact with others, but are still essentially alone in our unique experiences of life. As technology continues to improve, so will "virtual reality," until there may come a day when it is impossible to know for sure which world we are inhabiting. I find VR as fascinating as I do frightening; the applications for good are there for sure, but I hate to think of us as becoming ever-more-separated islands, with our headsets keeping us focused on ourselves and the lonely shows we are producing in our minds.

Sometimes I wonder if my whole life is part of someone else's dream…but then I realize. It is. It is part of God's dream for the world, and it is a dream of peace, and love, and joy. So as I make the choices that shape my reality, may I live into the big, baffling, beautiful pic-ture that our God created. May I stop fearing progress, and instead be exhilarated by wonderful newness. The future is here, now. And let me thank God for that.

WE ARE ONE

Bathed in beautiful golden light. Every haloed head staring out at us. Painted images laden with symbolism not grasped by the casual observer. These are icons, the icons adorning the little Albanian Orthodox church in Northeast Philadelphia I visited yesterday with our Confirmands. We watched as the congregation entered, kissing the icons as a sign of veneration. They also kissed the cross, and the chalice after they had communed…a lot of kissing. In the air hung the strong scent of incense. In our ears resonated the plaintive chanting of the a cappella choir, singing in English, Albanian and Russian. We tasted the blessed but unconsecrated bread of communion (consecrated is reserved for the faithful, swallowed on little spoons mixed with wine—even the babies partook). Before the Divine Liturgy, Father Nicholas talked with us, explaining the origins of the church and giving us hints of what we would soon experience. We came away with more questions for sure, but also a strong sense of this bedrock faith, from which sprang all of Christianity. The church members could not have been more welcoming, even though we almost outnumbered them. And in this close-knit, largely immigrant group of people, we were reminded that we all, too, were once recent arrivals to these shores, balancing our native cultures and the realities of this vast and daunting new land.

This was the 15th year of our "Exploring Faith Communities" series. We have taken our kids to learn, and worship, at Hindu temples and Muslim mosques. Centering ourselves in the blessed quiet of Quaker meeting. Meditating with Buddhists. Joyfully rocking the house at a North Philly African American church. And while we have traveled widely, we keep coming down to this: the values we share are greater than what divides us. Period.

I grew up Roman Catholic, in a time when we were strictly encouraged NOT to learn about other faiths. After all, we were in the right—why muddy things up with considering alternate viewpoints? But times have changed, and now more than ever, we are citizens of a great big, yet very small world. It is so important to try to understand each other, to care for each other. We seal ourselves off from our fellow man at our peril.

And so we find ourselves transported to this lovely, almost-heavenly landscape, watching and praying as the priest chants, his back to us at the altar. We chafe at first, and then we are told that the priest turns away in order to be one with us, pointing to God. So we surrender to the mysteries of Orthodox worship, and become part of that worship—just as we join our Baptist, our Mennonite, our UCC brothers and sisters. All of us holding lanterns to light each other's way through the darkness. So blessed to be part of a vast community of faith, whatever shape that faith may take. But all of us knowing that we stand in the presence of our multi-faceted, ever-loving God.

OR BEST OFFER

Our town of Oreland has an "online yard sale" Facebook page. Folks post pictures of items they are trying to sell, and people respond to them if interested. I've seen jewelry, bunk beds, sports equipment and clothing snapped up eagerly, and it's tempting to try and unload some of our treasures this way. But so far I have not participated, because I still have fresh recollections of many "real" yard sales we have had. We've had these every couple of years, because we've never learned.

It was such a good idea! Taking things we didn't need and turning them into cash! We would spend the night before each sale dusting everything off, labeling and pricing to beat the band. We were sure everybody was going to LOVE the assortment of costumes that had been donated to us for our theater company and we couldn't use. Think about it, who wouldn't kill for a giant bear suit? My collection of second-string cookbooks, including *The Canadiana Cookbook,* (which, if memory serves, had rather too many recipes featuring maple syrup) was also up for sale.

As the evening wore on, we always became greedy and started to price things higher and higher. My mother's wedding gifts (sterling silver platters so heavy they could double as murder weapons? Ka-ching!). Sterling is worth a fortune, isn't it? The Madame Alexander dolls? $50 each! No, $75!! We went to bed with visions of dollar signs dancing in our heads.

In the cold light of dawn, we set out our card tables and arranged our bounty. Everything looked a bit shabbier than it had the night before, but we were optimistic!! The first hint of trouble came before 8 AM when the "early birds" arrived. These canny shoppers canvassed the area every Saturday morning looking for bargains. They usually had specific items they were seeking, from musical instruments to vintage LPs. Even when we offered hot coffee, they passed right by our little assortment of stuff.

As the hours crept along customer-less, we were reminded of why we always did so poorly with yard sales—our stuff is either no good to begin with, or so badly maintained as to be almost worthless. In late afternoon, the giant bear suit would go out on a table marked "Free." My *Canadiana Cookbook* found a home with my wonderful Canadian neighbor, who most likely purchased it out of pity. No one wanted the Madame Alexander dolls; NO ONE wanted the tarnished sterling silver platters. In the end, we'd wasted an entire day and made just enough money to get a takeout pizza (no extra toppings) after we lugged things back inside.

Like the pain of labor, the memories would eventually fade, and we'd find ourselves doing it all over again.

My sister Carolyn has always made a bundle at her yard sales, perhaps because EVERYTHING she and her hubby Rob own is in mint condition. Who wouldn't do well selling a beautiful drum set and still-in-the-wrapper DVDs? It seems our daughter Julie is a chip off that block, because she is registered on the Oreland yard sale page and is doing very well. The old rabbit pen, ill-fitting shoes, never-opened nail polish (yes!)—all have been claimed quickly. Julie urges me to sell online as well, so the other day I rounded up some odds and ends to photograph and post. Haven't done it yet, though, because I'm sure our every knick-knack bears the Seyfried curse and will languish, embarrassingly unsold, forever.

Someday I'll go for it and mark down the few items we have that are worth anything, just for the thrill of a successful transaction. And afterward, as we stand counting our cash in our empty dining room (table and 8 chairs! $20! Or Best Offer!) we will figure out if we made enough money to go out and buy back our own table and (8) chairs, which will no doubt have been marked way, way up by a savvy yard sale-r. We will not pay a penny more than $200! After all, we have our pride!

AN OBSERVATION

"I never forget things. I just don't observe them in the first place."

—Bauvard

I am probably the most unobservant person you will ever meet. When someone asks me to describe anything, be it a person, a car or a house, I draw a total blank, and end up relying on the vaguest of comments (oh her? She's um, average looking! What does he drive? I would say a...you know... mid-size! What style of home? It's a...it's just lovely!). I have to stop and think about my kids' eye colors, the number of chairs in our family room, the names of the roads leading to the supermarket where I've shopped for over 30 years. Do you wear glasses? Have braces? How about a beard? Hmmm, let's see. Nope, I give up. If I ever played the game where someone leaves the room and changes something about themselves before returning, I'd have to just take a wild stab at guessing (did you have a cast on your arm? Did you just pierce your nose?) because I didn't notice what they looked like before they left. I guess these things are not important enough to me to stick, and it's a shame, because they ARE important.

The most recent example of something major I didn't see was my daughter-in-law's pregnancy. Ya-Jhu and Sheridan live with us, for Heaven's sake, we see them multiple times a day. Yaj was wearing looser clothes. She was quizzing me on my labors, asking me what I thought of different baby names...and I didn't have a clue. When my friend Deb Quaco flat out asked me if she was expecting, after having seen her a few days earlier, I responded with, "Pregnant? Yaj? Nooooooo, of course not." At that point, Ya-Jhu was already four months along. Chalk up another one missed for me!

Have you ever heard the phrase, "The devil is in the details"? Well, I believe it's God who is in the details, every last one. Every grain of sand, every tiny wildflower, every baby's fingernail—all bear the mark of our Creator. Even man-made things can be traced quickly back to the maker of the man (or woman). This whole beautiful universe is Divinely fashioned, from an infinity of solar systems right down to sub-atomic particles. And I race absent-mindedly through my days, neglecting to notice 99% of it.

So here's my Lenten discipline: I am trying to pay attention. I will do more than glance out the window to see if it's raining; I will go outside and turn my face up to each miraculous drop. I will look at the people I encounter, really look, and try much harder to retain the beauty of every individual soul. I will listen to a new piece of music, and not forget what it sounds like instantly after hearing. Because I have the great, great God-given gifts of my five senses, and I've been squandering them.

I'm not banking on a huge improvement right away. Don't ask me to draw a map of my neighborhood, or even an accurate picture of my office—I'll probably still flunk. But I am trying my best to really "observe" Lent this year, and hopefully I can continue to be more mindful, in general, all year long.

BAREFOOTIN'

That's the name of my good friend Dennis Forney's weekly column. Dennis is the editor of the *Cape Gazette*, the wonderful newspaper down here in Lewes, Delaware. Dennis is a terrific journalist, and always unearths fascinating stories of local residents and history. Over the years, Den and I have had some great conversations about life, literature, music and faith, among many other topics. A native of the Eastern Shore of the Chesapeake Bay, Dennis has traveled a good bit, but in his heart he has never strayed far from his roots.

Over 30-plus years of friendship, Dennis has always looked just the same to me: tall, tan, lean, sporting an Amish-style beard, an ever-present baseball cap and yes, much of the time, bare feet. Dennis is probably the most recognizable figure in this beach town. And I sometimes wonder what that would be like.

For you see, I grew up pretty root-less. I am a native New Yorker but feel like a bit of a fraud when I revisit because I have retained so few childhood connections to the Big Apple. My time in Atlanta in late elementary school and high school brought more solid friendships, but still no heart-connection to the place (and, to be fair, Atlanta changes its face as often as a plastic-surgery-addicted socialite). During our early years of marriage, Steve and I lived on the road, touring the South in dinner theatre productions and then the

Northeast with children's theatre. We never unpacked our bags, we belonged to no zip code.

It wasn't until we settled in Oreland in 1986 that I ever felt settled, period. And now, nearly 30 years later, I still don't truly feel like a "local." Some of that for sure is that other Orelanders tend to have lived here (or close by) for generations. But also? I have never truly invested my heart here. In the back of my mind, I have always had my bags packed in anticipation of another move somewhere down the road. I love my friends and neighbors for sure, but Acme Supermarket and Rosario's Pizza do not inspire any sentimentality.

Lewes in the summer comes closer than Philly, because of the decades of happy summer memories with our kids, but I would still never call myself a "local." By now at age 58, whether we stay nearby or pick up stakes and move to Tahiti, I am sure I will always feel as if I am just passing through, wherever we end up.

So do I envy Dennis? On some level, sure I do. His geography helps define him, and he is an integral part of his community in many ways. I have no such local identity. Whoever writes my obituary someday will have a hard time saying where I am really from. Steve is in the same boat, with a good bit of Indiana and south Georgia in the mix of his background. And our offspring? Well, they can definitely say they all grew up in Oreland. However, I will be shocked if ANY of them end up staying here permanently. To a person, they are already world travelers, and I don't see that changing anytime soon.

Jesus was a hometown boy from Nazareth. Now, He didn't stay there forever. He had places to go and people to see, and teach, and heal. But I do think of Him as a very recognizable local character there, though: the carpenter's kid. Barefootin', as it were. The guy everyone knew. And the thing is, when you are that well known, there is nowhere to hide. Your integrity is wrapped up in your geography. I truly believe our Lord would be just as perfect, just as sterling a character, even if He had been an anonymous big-city dweller, but for many people keeping a low profile has its advantages. Flaws can slip by undetected. There is some measure of self-protection when you are not too famous. Or so we think.

Bottom line though? The world is one big hometown, and God is the mayor. He knows us all intimately, warts and all, and while there is nowhere to hide from Him, there is no need, either. We are as well-known, and well loved, to God as Dennis is to the people of Lewes, and even more so.

So maybe I shouldn't worry about where I'm from, because deep down I know. I know who I am and whose I am. Oreland or Lewes or New York or Atlanta, it's all the same. I am, we are, locals, in the very best sense of that word.

Howdy, neighbor!

IN JULIE'S BACKPACK

Julie has worn backpacks since preschool days. The early ones were festooned with cartoon characters and held miniscule amounts of stuff (small backs can only tote so much, after all). In elementary school she graduated to sturdy packs from L.L. Bean with her monogram on them; these were so pricey that they were made to last until they were in tatters. The beginning of middle school and high school warranted the purchase of new backpacks, these weighing so much that it seemed she must have gone out to the yard and filled them with rocks—but no, it was just American History, Biology and Algebra I, their pages bulging with facts and figures to memorize. I no longer automatically checked the contents of her bag for notes from teachers, because the age of emails and texts and class webpages had dawned, and there were much more efficient ways for me to be contacted.

As I watched Jules hoist her mammoth sack onto her still petite frame and trudge out to the bus stop, I would flash back to the little red Sesame Street number she had sported at age four. At those moments I would yearn for the years when her life, like her backpack, was an open book. These days, Julie carried in her pack a cell phone filled with friends' numbers, and a wallet stuffed with spending money from her first job, as a waitress in a retirement community.

After high school Julie had special backpack plans. She had her heart set on, and gradually convinced her father and me about, taking a gap year to work and travel. She painstakingly mapped out a three-month European backpacking trek, mostly solo, and saved diligently to fund her adventure. Some people were shocked that we agreed to let her go, but those who knew Jules well knew that she was as responsible as a 30 year old. She would stay in youth hostels, punctuating her trip with longer stays with her brother Patrick in Germany, and our former exchange student Maurus, who lived with his family in Switzerland.

And so it was that I found myself in the Newark, NJ airport on an afternoon in late August, preparing to bid my youngest child farewell. In my hand I held a printed-out copy she'd given me of her 11 country itinerary, complete with the addresses and phone numbers of her every scheduled stop. In my heart, I held her promise that we would touch base every day. We snapped photos of our intrepid girl with her newest—and largest yet—backpack, a huge pack from REI. If I had looked into this backpack, I would have beheld a sensible amount of all-weather clothing, a laptop, a Kindle. This would be her portable headquarters for the next 90 days, and would accompany her from plane to train to bus, from Rome to Paris to Vienna.

Could I have climbed into Julie's backpack that day? If I could have, I surely would have, nestling among the tee shirts and toiletries. I would have held my breath and made myself as light as a feather, so that I would not burden her. But I would have been there, to wander through the cathedrals and museums and city streets with her, to offer her hugs, and company, and extra protection in new places.

She finally turned away from us and joined the line for security, passport and boarding pass in hand. From our angle, all we could see was a giant backpack with legs, moving farther and farther away from us every second. There would be no traveling together this time, and I knew it—just as I could never have folded myself into her Elmo backpack, among the cookie crumbs and crayon drawings. It would have been too tight a squeeze to be wedged between her Geography and Environmental Science textbooks. Even if I offered to hold her phone and wallet, to bring along containers of sesame noodles and cocoa bars, my help would not have been needed or welcomed. I would simply have weighed too much.

I was never made to fit into Julie's backpack, much as I might wish to. I could only tuck a note in there, sending her off across the ocean with all my love and all my hope (and maybe a little of my fear too). Her mother could not travel with her, but I finally recognized that Julie's backpack was just the perfect size for her, and always had been.

SOUNDTRACK OF MY LIFE

I never sing around the house. Oh, sure, when the kids were babies I would warble the odd tune, but as soon as they were out of diapers the concert was over. I don't hum, either, so unless I am yapping (which is admittedly often), I am silent. And I've often wondered why. But then I remember my mom, and it all comes clear.

Ours was a noisy house, and while we girls fighting accounted for some of the cacophony, the main culprit was our mother Joanie. Her every activity was accompanied by song, and when she wasn't singing she was humming. The louder the hum, the more annoying she found the chore to be (when she was ironing it sounded like the rumble of thunder). She sang when happy, sad and everything in between. And her repertoire? Nary a children's song in the bunch. Instead, we were treated to the music of the 1940's. "Summertime," "All of Me" and my personal favorite, "Two Sleepy People," which contained lyrics like 'Here we are/out of cigarettes/holding hands and yawning/look how late it gets.' For Mom, being out of cigarettes would be unbearably sad, so she would sing that one in a more mournful tone.

As a result of listening to Mom's own personal Hit Parade, my sisters and I knew most of the Rodgers and Hart catalogue, with some Cole Porter and Gershwin thrown in for good measure. When musical tastes changed, she did not; I couldn't imagine her ever tackling

Elvis or the Beatles. I think the era of her songs was the happiest time in her life in a lot of ways, and singing them brought those good feelings back.

Joanie's years as a "career girl" sounded impossibly fun and glamorous to us little girls, almost like a movie (a musical, of course). She worked in New York City for years before she met Dad, and we always heard tales about her escapades as a secretary. She worked in the radiology department at Lenox Hill Hospital (for a Dr. John Miller, who later died of cancer from exposure to X-rays). Next she was a secretary at NBC in the exciting early days of television (think The Today Show when it was hosted by Dave Garroway and his un-likely chimpanzee co-star, J. Fred Muggs).

Mom's love life was a busy one indeed, filled with fabulous nights on the town in Manhattan, dinner and dancing with many handsome and charming dates. There was an ill-fated romance with a (gasp) Protestant (her family was staunchly Catholic), and I will always believe that he was the love of her life. Very shortly after that relationship ended, Mom suddenly jumped into marriage at age 29, to a man she had only known a few months. Mom and Dad's wed-ding, followed almost immediately by back-to-back pregnancies, was a stunningly rapid life change for her. That she loved her three daughters deeply I have no doubt, but there was no mistaking her wistfulness whenever she recalled her young single days gone by.

Ten years ago, Mom died in our house, peacefully, at the age of 80, after a short illness. She knew her end was coming, and was able to say goodbye to all five of her beloved grandkids. My sister Carolyn and I took turns staying by her bedside all night so she'd never be alone. And when the time for singing was done, there was still a serenade left: Evan had recorded himself playing her favorite tunes on the piano, and that was all she wanted to listen to. And so, the soundtrack of my life, accompanied her into Heaven.

Sometimes I regret not singing to my children, but I know that's not me. It was, however, my mother. And when I miss Joanie, which is very often, I can listen to "My Funny Valentine" and feel her presence, still.

NEW ORLEANS, REVISITED

This week, in honor of Patrick and Meg's second anniversary of dating, and Meg's birthday, they flew to New Orleans for a short vacation. They both work incredibly hard, and I am really tickled that they were able to make this getaway happen. New Orleans happens to be one of my favorite cities, so I enjoyed hearing about their plans. As I listened, the years fell away, and I was back in 1981, and my first time in NOLA.

I took the train (the old Southern Crescent) from Philly, and was visiting my good friend Lisa, who was working at the Times-Picayune newspaper. I had recently fallen during a performance of "The Wizard of Oz" (darn that slippery Yellow Brick Road!) and broken my wrist; I was in a cast halfway up my right arm. Since I am left handed, I could navigate fairly well—still able to enjoy a Café du Monde beignet and café au lait, so the important things happened! I heard some amazing jazz and Cajun music at the Maple Leaf Bar, ate at locals' favorite places including Buster Holmes, Roussel's and Mother's, and attended Easter Sunday Mass at St. Louis Cathedral.

The city made a major impression on me—its beauty, the music, the food—so much so that I returned the following year with Steve, and we had an equally delightful time (with Lisa again as our gracious hostess). Within 18 months I became pregnant with the first of our five, thus ending our child-free jaunts for quite a few years.

New Orleans was dead, almost exactly 13 years ago. A wall of water drenched this city, water 6 feet deep that didn't drain for 3 weeks. Water that left a stench that lasted for 2 years. Water that washed away hope, washed away livelihoods, washed away some of what made New Orleans the most unique and wonderful city in America. Water peeled the surface away, and exposed the poorest, neediest of its citizens. People who were barely scraping by before Katrina, and were totally devastated in her wake. Many, many of those people are gone; a large percentage of the pre-Katrina population cannot return. Then there were the people who were still trying to rebuild their lives, who haven't stayed gone, who believed that New Orleans would rise again.

I always hoped for another chance to spend time in the Garden District and the French Quarter, and in 2009, I was finally able to go back, this time chaperoning 30 teenagers at the Lutheran National Youth Gathering. I was eager to introduce two of my kids (Patrick and Julie) to New Orleans. 28 years had passed, and the extensive damage from Hurricane Katrina four years before was still very apparent in many neighborhoods. Our group spent a day painting the water-damaged house of a couple who had evacuated to Baton Rouge. Even after the disaster, they were determined to come home to their beloved city.

A highlight of the 2009 visit had been a cruise on the Mississippi River aboard the steamboat Natchez. Yesterday, Meg and Patrick took a cruise on the same boat, which still runs daily excursions. They will be having brunch at Brennan's (a 1981 brunch stop for me), and of course hit Café du Monde. They're having great fun, and I'm so glad to know the city is back on its feet at last.

In a country where most metropolitan areas have become sadly similar, with their downtown high rises and their ubiquitous chain restaurants and hotels, New Orleans is one of the few cities that remains proudly unique. May it always be so, and may Mother Nature be kinder in the future to the Big Easy, a place that has come to mean such a lot to me.

PERSONALITY PLUS

I've been avoiding taking those silly Facebook quizzes (Which Harry Potter Character Are You?), recognizing that they shed little light on who I am. After more than ten years of psychotherapy, I still have no more than a nodding acquaintance with myself. I was actually relieved to be diagnosed with a mental illness, so that when asked about the workings of my inner self, saying "Oh, I'm bipolar!" would cover it.

In my heart I know that human beings are far more complicated than any test can really assess. But that doesn't stop people from taking them. For a while there, the Myers-Briggs Type Indicator Test, which sorts people into one of 16 types, was THE big personality evaluator. After taking the test, you would be identified with four letters (E-extroversion, I-introversion; T-thinking, F-feeling, etc.). Everyone I knew, it seemed, would tell me that they were ESFJs, or INTPs, or whatever. Because this alphabet soup was so popular with my friends and colleagues, I feigned familiarity with it (though I never actually took the test). When asked my score, I would respond, "Me? Oh, I'm a QWERTYUIOP!" then duck out before my questioner realized I had just recited the top line of the typing keyboard.

So why did I just take the trendy Big Five personality test? After all these years, I was curious, more than anything else. What amazing new insights about Elise Seyfried might be uncovered? The

Big Five (acronym OCEAN) are Openness to New Experiences, Conscientiousness, Extroversion, Agreeableness and (my fave) Neuroticism. I was excited! Would I finally have a handle on "me" after 60 years?

My results:

O (Openness) Seems I am NOT very open to new experiences. True. From zip lining in Costa Rica to parallel parking in Philly, "no thank you" is my go-to reaction. Give me my comfy old experiences every time! I never tire of re-reading my favorite books, re-watching my favorite movies, re-eating my favorite meals. If you only live once, I am perfectly happy to spend my one life repeating myself.

C (Conscientiousness) I am neither organized, nor disorganized. Also true. I am careful about my appearance, and can pull things together at work well enough. Yet beneath the façade is chaos, chaos I tell you! I am a closet slob (meaning, if you open my closets you will learn that I am a slob).

E (Extroversion) Apparently I am relatively social and enjoy the company of others. To this I say: what others? I do not enjoy the company of just any "others." And my general sociability ebbs and flows; some days I am Ginny Gregarious, and some days I would rather converse with my pillow (these are GREAT conversations, in which my opinion always wins the day).

A (Agreeableness) I am (by their rating) not extremely agreeable. Hmmm. I do recall my little grudges, my petty annoyances. I was often irked by my in-laws, because I hated their complacence and lack of intellectual curiosity. Once, we were watching a game show on TV together and playing along. The contestants were asked the question: would you rather be smart and unhappy, or dumb and happy? Guess which one I chose? Smart and unhappy, of course! Guess which one they chose? Dumb and happy! What on earth was the matter with them? Now, many years later, I am much more understanding of Mom and Dad Seyfried, and am starting at last to see the value of "happy" in this crazy world.

N (Neuroticism) I am a "generally anxious person and tend to worry about everything." Hmmm. Well. Yes. But why on earth would that be called "neurotic"? To me, that is a totally normal reaction to life. Besides, if nobody worried, many many more bad things would happen! Worry keeps the devil at bay! You're welcome!

So how should I deal with these revealing results? Should I work on my conscientiousness, my openness, my extroversion? Should I strive to be more agreeable, less neurotic? In other words, is knowledge power?

Nah. I wanted to learn about me. I never said I would actually DO anything about me. But now that I know who I am, I think I'll check out those Facebook quizzes again, just for fun. What Flavor of Ice Cream AM I? Can't wait to find out!

THE ENVELOPE, PLEASE

> "I want to unfold. I don't want to stay folded any-
> where, because where I am folded, there I am a lie."
>
> --Rainier Maria Rilke

Opening the envelope at awards ceremonies is always a dramatic moment. The truth (the winner) is revealed (though once in a while mistakes are made—see Oscars, 2016). The contents of the envelope are a secret to us until the moment of revelation, at which point we say either "I knew it! Yay!" or "I cannot believe it! Boo!" Before that, though, all is mystery. Without being opened, the envelope has no meaning.

I love getting letters, rare as they are in this digital age. Just the act of opening the envelope and unfolding the message thrills me. As I read, it feels like the author has opened him or her self to me, with words for my eyes only. If the letter had stayed folded up, I'd never know what my friend was saying to me. It would be closed off, and useless to me as a means of communication. But I unfold the paper, and I learn.

While I like to think of myself as an open book (or unfolded piece of paper, as it were), in reality I am pretty darned folded, down into the smallest package possible. My favored sleeping position is fetal; I have always hated lying on my back because it feels too exposed.

When I am sick or afraid, I clench my fists, turn in on myself and burrow down. Even in good times, I tend to fold up my insecurities and flaws, so that I can present a creased and tidy parcel to the world.

In Anne Lamott's wonderful new book, *Hallelujah Anyway*, she talks about folding and unfolding ourselves. She says, "We got folded by trying as hard as we could to make everyone happy…we agreed to get folded at school and in jobs, to get ahead…self-importance fueled by performance anxiety, people-pleasing, sloth and bad self-esteem, wrapped us into small crisp squares like professionally laundered shirts." And the key to life, Lamott tells us, is to UNfold, expose ourselves to the elements, whatever they may be. To be vulnerable and open, and thus able to receive God's grace and mercy.

At my age and stage of life, I am finally tired of being folded like an origami frog (whimsical as they may be). I have enough natural wrinkles that I do not need to give myself any more. But it's scary, this unfolding business, and I'm not sure I can really do it. While over the years my folded-up self has been hurt plenty, in the back of my mind I always think exposing my true self would have made things worse.

But I'm trying. Down here at the shore, I am taking a yoga class twice a week, early in the mornings on the beach. I realized that my least favorite part of my yoga practice has been "corpse pose" (shavasana), the time at the end when all we do is stretch out flat on our towels. Eyes closed, I've been imagining green-head flies stinging me, or, worse, receiving unwanted "gifts" from seagulls overhead. If only I could curl up in a ball, I think, I'd protect myself!

Last Thursday, at the end of class, I lay on my back as usual, but this time I didn't focus on what could go wrong. Instead, I focused on sinking into the sand, becoming one with the beautiful sunny morning. Amazingly, I felt a rush of joy and freedom, so much so that I stretched my arms out over my head, as vulnerable as I could possibly be. And in that openness, I felt the presence of God, who has been patiently there all along, waiting for me to unclench and experience the Divine.

Folded-up letters in envelopes do no one any good. It is in the unfolding, in the reading and sharing, that letters have life. So in these beautiful but fleeting, waning days of summer, God grant me the courage to unfold myself, flaws and all, and dare to experience life to the fullest—the good and the not-so-good both. And may my life be an open letter of love and hope and encouragement for every person who reads it.

CHEZ NANA

I can still smell her scorched toast, and see her scraping off the blackened surface, topping it with dollops of orange marmalade. That, with canned fruit cocktail and Sara Lee coffeecake, was breakfast chez Nana. Her husband, Pop, favored a different morning menu: cold canned baked beans, strawberry ice cream, several cigars, a shot and a beer. That was just one of the many differences between them, and even as a little girl I recognized that they were ill-matched. But I took it as just a fact of life; it wasn't until years later that I felt sorry for Nana, sorry that she could not ever bring herself to leave the man who enjoyed calling her BFLOW (Big Fat Lazy Old Woman).

Pop always declared he would not eat cheese, and made a huge deal out of it. Therefore, for the entirety of their marriage, Nana challenged herself to sneak cheese into almost everything he ate, from mashed potatoes to scrambled eggs. She got a secret charge out of watching him wolf down chicken salad with tiny cubes of Velveeta and banana pudding with cream cheese, even as he was loudly proclaiming his refusal to even taste that particular dairy product. The Stealth Cheese Project was Nana's small revenge for the years of marital misery inflicted on her by my grandfather.

Cheesy shenanigans aside, Nana hated to cook. When we, her beloved granddaughters, stayed for dinner at their apartment, Nana would try her best to prepare something edible for us. As the smoke billowed behind her, she would emerge from her kitchenette with a platter of charred gray meat tied with twine (the challenge was to differentiate the roast whatever-it-was from the string), plop some mushy canned carrots (with cheese!) on plates and announce that dinner was served. We would saw away at the entrée, and manage to chew a few dry mouthfuls before declaring that we were "done".

Of course, we weren't that hungry anyway, not after snack time. Nana lived just a few blocks from our Manhattan Catholic elementary school, and would pick us up once or twice a week. As soon as we got off the elevator, we would ask if we were having Ring Dings or Devil Dogs that day. Nana was as big a fan of those preservative-laden pre-packaged delights as we were, so soon there were just chocolate crumbs and cellophane wrappers left from our after-school indulgence. The beverages of choice were Hawaiian Punch (which came in Red and Yellow) and Hi-C. My teeth still hurt from the memory of all that sugar.

One year, after we had moved South, we were up visiting our grandparents in New York. During our stay, I got the flu. I couldn't keep anything down for days, and Nana was extremely worried that I would waste away. So she was constantly in the bedroom, trying to tempt me with her take on invalid food. Chicken broth and saltines and ginger ale in little sips? Not for Nana! As soon as I showed any signs of appetite, in came a tray with cream of chicken soup, a huge, mayonnaise-y ham sandwich, and a big glass of Coke. Needless to say, that meal's time in my upset stomach was short-lived. But I knew it was her love offering, so I ate it anyway, because that was my love offering to her.

By her late sixties, Nana, who for years had carried too much extra weight, and whose idea of exercise was waving her hand to hail a taxi, began her physical decline. She developed diabetes, and was sternly told by her doctors to change her habits. But she persisted in swallowing gallons of her favorite Hawaiian Punch, in eating whatever food was the most un-healthy. In the end, it was a heart attack that got her, when I was 13 years old. Pop, the bane of her existence, managed to outlive her by a year and a half.

I often wonder if my weird relationship with diet in the years that followed stemmed in part from watching Nana's literal death by chocolate. I resented the Yodels that took her away from me. As a teenager, I seesawed between going on starvation regimes of water and hard-boiled eggs, and learning to cook complicated dishes with only the freshest ingredients. To this day, I shun pre-packaged anything, and don't eat snacks. To this day, I think about food too much, and wrestle with its too-prominent place in my life.

But now that I'm 61, I think of Nana tenderly. She coped with her difficult life as best she could, in a time when striking out on her own would not have been supported by her church. She expressed the love she had for me and my sisters by feeding us the things she loved herself. And if she died too early, I no longer blame the food, or her.

And so this morning, I turn the toaster up high, in fond memory of my Nana. And as I scrape the burned bread, I see her scraping too, making the best of a bad situation. I spread on marmalade as she did, and taste the bittersweetness. I can't look back on delicious times in my grandmother's kitchen, but I can recall the happiness she gave me, and her love on every plate.

WHAT WORLD CUP?

I have no excuse—except perhaps for my profound hatred of the sound of the vuvuzela. I missed the entire World Cup, the excitement of the games and all the attendant hoopla. Totally blew it off. Didn't see a single goal scored by anyone. Oh, I read about it, after the fact. But I missed the chance to cheer, along with the rest of the world, for an impressive array of international sports teams. Maybe I'll do better next time, but I rather doubt it—although Ann Coulter recently said that enjoying soccer was un-American, her blathering reason enough for me to decide to love the game.

My other misses this year include the NCAA college basketball tournament (which came and went without me viewing basket #1, even as my family printed out brackets and scribbled their guesses), the World Series, and the entire NFL season. And my ignorance extended to the Oscars, Tonys and Emmys...all very widely-seen programs, except by me. Who was in the National League playoffs? The Final Four? Who took home the statuette for Best Actress in a Musical? Only the internet clued me in, the next day.

Yesterday was the 45th anniversary of the first moon walk by Neil Armstrong. I was 12, and remember it well—the thrill of watching history being made, feeling part of a world-wide audience all focused on the same thing. Many of the other pivotal moments (9/11 comes to mind) that I have viewed on TV have been tragic, but I still took some comfort in knowing that millions of others were glued to the same images, praying as I was. Nowadays, I'm feeling so overwhelmed that I've been opting out of focusing on major world events of any kind.

I always think of the world as much more manageably sized in Jesus' time, so many fewer people and places of note. So much less to grasp, to be up on. And there are times I wish our civilization was smaller, so that we could understand more of it. But then I remember that life was just as hard to understand back then, and the world seemed just as vast and unknowable. And I recall that Jesus didn't travel all that widely during His time on earth—St. Paul covered much more territory. The point was that He made every step count, paying attention to the smallest details about the people and situations He encountered.

And Jesus came here to serve as a model for us, all people in all times and places. With so very much going on, every minute, everywhere, it is easy to feel swamped and to just turn it all off. We are over-saturated with information, from war in the Middle East to atrocities in the Ukraine, right down (way down) to day-by-day updates on the Kardashian clan. How to sort it out? How to ride the tidal wave of stuff with which we are bombarded, without drowning?

The answer may just be to start small and local, as Jesus did. To get to know our neighbors and their needs, the problems of our own cities and towns. To pay attention to details, and find the threads that connect us all. And then, as we reach out beyond, to find the events and causes we can be passionate about, and focus on them. Knowing that we can't do it all, be everywhere, care equally about everything. That's all right, because we are not alone. There are billions of us on this planet, and if even a fraction of us can take action, the world can become a much, much better place.

So if I have become overwhelmed by mega-events, may I not lose interest in the micro-events that fill my days, the people who populate my life. May I stay informed about the state of our civilization as best I can, and do what I can to make a difference globally, but also remember to value my interactions with my little corner of the world.

After all, that's what Jesus did.

HOLIDAY FOLLIES

Attention Back Friday Shoppers! You know who you are. Your idea of rip-roaring fun is lining up in the chilly, pre-dawn hours the day after Thanksgiving in front of Best Buy or Target or Walmart in order to snag the Door Buster Specials. You have a list on your iPhone, and you cross-check prices with similar Internet offerings as you barrel down the aisles. You're the kind that has every single Christmas present wrapped, labeled and ready to go a month (or more) in advance—and you always come in under budget. I admire your energy, especially if you are also the one who pulled off that ridiculous 27 course turkey dinner the day before. Kudos to you, as you staggered in your front door, heavy laden with shopping bags. Now you can relax for a bit, no?

Nope. It's now time for you to craft the ultimate family Christmas card and accompanying letter, often titled "Latest from the Longabergers!" or "Ho Ho Ho from the Haberdasher Clan!" In past years, my mailbox would be crammed with the fruits of your labors for weeks ahead of December 25th. You were the prescient one who thought to photograph your entire family on the beach the previous summer, dressed all matchy matchy in your white pants and blue denim shirts! The voluminous update accompanying this lovely picture would tell the glad tidings of weddings, graduations, vacation extravaganzas, new houses and new babies.

The alternative missive, of course, was the Epic Tale of Woe: *"It's been an interesting year. We lost Uncle Bernie in June (he didn't die, we just lost track of him). An unfortunate blowtorch accident put an end to Mom Mom's crème brulee business. Bob and I struggle along: cataract surgery, arthritis, psoriasis, and dual hip replacements. Fun-filled holidays to you and yours!!"*

Nowadays, more and more of these masterpieces are sent via email or Facebook, and Mr. or Ms. Post Person doesn't have quite so much to do. But you still manage to far outshine those of us who lost our Christmas card address list back in 2003 (that would include yours truly), and haven't sent a Yuletide greeting since.

I come by my planning-averse personality naturally. There's the oft-heard family story of my poor sister Maureen's sixth birthday, Saturday, Nov. 23, 1963. Mom tended to wait and hit the stores on the birthday itself, and as that was the day after JFK's assassination, every store in New York City was closed. Sad as we all were about that tragic event, little Mo was sadder still, with no gifts to open until the following week.

I don't wait quite that late to shop, but I come pretty close. And on the rare occasions when I do plan ahead, I can never remember where I hid my finds when it comes time to deliver the goods (this just happened the other day, as I scoured the house in search of a gift I had bought for daughter Julie at her favorite Rehoboth boutique last summer). So it may be for the best that my holiday shopping doesn't occur too far ahead of time. My formula for success? Sending husband Steve out to the mall every Christmas Eve with a list (he doesn't mind—or so he says), and, of course, the blessing of Amazon Prime. "Want it tomorrow? Order in the next two hours and 47 minutes" and there I am, frantically entering my credit card numbers, two hours and 46 minutes later.

So I hope you had a ball on Black Friday, über-organized friends! Enjoyed the crazy crowds, the thrill of the chase, the satisfaction of a job well done? Good for you! I was sitting right here, idly scrolling through your perfect Turkey Day family photos on my computer as I realize we forgot to take any! Fun-filled Holidays to All!

NEVER GIVE UP!

I've been feeling a bit discouraged lately about submitting my essays to various contests and publications, which would make sense if I was getting a pile of rejections. But I'm not. I sent one piece to one place and never heard back. Yet I always assume that, not only is a newspaper or magazine passing on my work, but the editor has passed my feeble effort around the office: "Hey guys, get a load of this! Hope she hasn't quit her day job!" Faced with this (admittedly far-fetched) prospect, I decide to keep my work safely on my own computer. They can't turn down what they never see, am I right?

But the past few months have reminded me that, for those who are determined to succeed, setbacks are an inevitable part of the process.

In February, I had the great pleasure of attending a concert with Julie, by the New York Philharmonic at Lincoln Center. I would have enjoyed the NY Phil had they been playing an orchestration of "Chopsticks," but this was a dream program: Beethoven's First Piano Concerto and Gustav Mahler's First Symphony. I love Beethoven, but I ADORE Mahler. His sweeping compositions create a world of their own, a cascade of varied and brilliant musical ideas that somehow fit perfectly together. I recalled that Mahler had himself conducted the US premiere of this symphony, by this orchestra, in New York in 1909. What I had forgotten was the almost universal panning the piece had gotten from music critics when it was first performed in

Europe. He never gave up, reworking it until it reached its final, triumphant form years later. Had Mahler pulled an Elise, the world would have forever been deprived of what has become a beloved masterwork.

In my own home, I watched as my baby grandson learned to crawl, then stand. Soon he will be walking. Peter is very young to be approaching this milestone, but that is not stopping him from trying. His tireless efforts have yet to produce that first step. Again, if Peter took after his Nana, he would still just be lying on his quilt, assuming that magically one day movement would happen. But he persists, with no frustrated tears—even when he ends up flat on his face, again. One day, quite soon, his efforts will pay off, and we will have another little walking man around the house.

Pastor Hy has, after many years of capably leading the Tuesday morning Bible study, retired. Ready or not, I am now running the show. We are looking at the Gospel of Mark, and as we do I am reminded that I was born Catholic, and back then Catholics NEVER read the Bible. Our only copy of Sacred Scripture at home was Mom and Dad's wedding Bible, in which my sisters and I colored with crayons.

As a church worker, my learning curve has been as steep as Mt. Everest. I teach Confirmation. I lead the first grade Bible workshop. In recent years I have been writing devotions, skits and plays for various religious publishers, all grounded in the Word of the Lord. At every turn, I discover something new. Catholics are taught that Jesus was an only child, but apparently he had siblings! I kinda figured Noah's Ark and the Garden of Eden were not literally true, but it's been a revelation (get it?) to read Bible scholars and get some historical background, when these stories may have been first told, and what they were meant to convey.

While I don't reach for it when I am seeking some light reading before bed, my Bible is looking a little tattered these days, a sign that it is in frequent use. I intend to keep plugging along, learning more and more about my faith—even if I am destined to stay just one step ahead of my students.

So what am I learning from a favorite composer, my beloved grandbaby, and my Bible adventures? Three little, but oh-so-important words: never give up! My essays may be rejected for a while, but maybe not forever. The only true failure is not persevering.

It's Sunday afternoon, and I am looking at several of my recent pieces which are languishing on my laptop. I think I'm going to send my literary babies out, today, and just see what happens. They may be rejected outright, but I can't worry about that. There are so many publications out there, after all. May I keep trying, and have faith that my audience is somewhere out there too.

TRIP PLANNER

Do you know what you'll be doing exactly five months from now?

I do. I will be en route to Ireland, with my two 20-something daughters. This is a 60th birthday gift, and I can't wait. Ever since I snagged cheap airline tickets, I have been after the girls to sit down with me and plan our itinerary. While they seem to be excited, they have strangely little interest in mapping out the details. "Relax, Mom!" they say. "Let's just wing it—be spontaneous!" Foolish young women! There is no spontaneity in successful vacations! Mind you, I've only taken a handful of vacations in my whole life, but whenever I HAVE gone away, the trips have been scripted to the millisecond.

Rose and Julie, on the other hand, have been very lucky indeed to have had good travel experiences, with minimal forethought. So what if they've made friends everywhere they've gone, and have lots of funny stories to tell about their missed trains, closed museums, and sketchy youth hostels? Friends and funny stories are NOT why you travel!

When Evan was an officer on a nuclear submarine out of Pearl Harbor, Hawaii, I visited him. There, my days were my own to micromanage, because Evan was working. Every morning, I would drop him off at the base and use his car for solo excursions around Oahu. My handy guidebooks at the ready, I ticked off my "must-do" experiences: hike Diamond Head, snorkel in Haunama Bay. I was so determined to eat a malasada (a famed local pastry) at Leonard's in Honolulu that I drove around in circles for 30 minutes looking for parking. And I couldn't find indoor seating. And it was raining. But by gum I ate that soggy donut, and convinced myself that it was worth every penny.

My 40th wedding anniversary trip to Paris and Barcelona was similarly über-planned. I was armed with multiple copies of guidebooks for both cities. Before my husband Steve and I even left home, I had gone online and bought a gourmet picnic lunch to be delivered to us at the Eiffel Tower. I couldn't be sure we would actually find edible food just roaming around in the world's gastronomic capital! Evan was now out of the Navy and in grad school in Barcelona, so he was one source of info (though what did he really know? He'd only lived there a year!). I looked up every single cathedral and eatery he suggested before we went, just to be on the safe side.

I'm trying to play it cool this time, and keep my investigating under wraps. I send the girls links to promising Bed & Breakfasts, but have only booked one so far. Well, two. OK, three. I have tagged possible lodgings for all the other nights, but haven't booked them. Yet. But the (economy size, automatic transmission) car is reserved, from one of the most reliable places in the whole country (according to a blog post I found, aptly titled "A Comprehensive Guide to Renting a Car in Ireland"). And I know exactly where to enjoy real Irish food and hear authentic Irish music, wherever we end up going. I will pretend to leave these choices to my offspring, though I will have researched hours and menus and lineups of musicians exhaustively. "Oh my, look!" I will say offhandedly as I direct the car towards one of my finds. "There is a random pub across this random road! I am guessing it might possibly serve the finest Irish Stew in all of County Meath! What say we give it a try? We don't have to, of course. Totally up to you."

If I play my cards right, I can spend hours every day for the next five months preparing for this trip—and make it look as if I did nothing at all. And as my daughters praise me for hanging loose for a change, I will accept their kudos. After all, this IS "hanging loose"—for me.

BY THE SEA

For the past 33 years, I have been lucky enough to live in coastal Delaware during the summers. Even though I work there, between doing church work via computer and helping at the Rehoboth Summer Children's Theatre, I still feel blessed by my proximity to the water. It's always there, in any weather, and I can scoot down for a quick walk on the beach anytime.

Lewes is perfectly situated where the Delaware Bay meets the Atlantic Ocean, with easy access to both. The bay is ever calm, and often features a sandbar yards from shore. When the kids were little, this was my beach of choice, because they could play in the shallows with no danger of big waves. Nowadays, I walk by the bay because I love to watch the sailboat races from the yacht club, to enjoy the next generation of children cavorting with their pails and shovels as they scoop up conch shells and even tiny horseshoe crabs.

But there are days when nothing but the majestic ocean will do. I stand, only venturing to get my feet wet, and marvel at the sparkle of the morning sun on the swirling surf. I am equally thrilled and terrified to watch braver folks than me riding the waves in with surf-boards and boogie boards. Past the tide break, dolphins leap from the sea, lovely and playful. Silhouetted against the brilliant sky, paddle-boarders stand and skim over the water so gracefully.

As is beautifully stated in Psalm 23, "He restores my soul." "He" is the incredible God of all creation, and the work of His hands, specifically the water, does indeed restore my soul, a soul that often reaches July totally exhausted and emptied out.

I attend Epworth United Methodist Church in the summers, and the pastor, Pat Loughlin, is a dear, dear friend. The other week, Pat preached on "Ocean". She talked about the passage in Matthew when Jesus walked on the water, and about Peter's literal leap of faith as he got out of the boat to meet Him. Pat said that the ocean asks us who we are, what is important to us, and what we are going to do about it. The big questions, appropriate for such a huge force of nature. The passage ends with the disciples saying, "Truly you are the Son of God." (Matthew 14:33) When I stand on the sand, do I feel the same assurance? Do I see Jesus walking on the water, reaching out His hand to me? It's all well and good to feel recharged by the beach, but am I <u>changed</u> by the beach? Do I step out beyond just wet feet, and risk submerging myself completely? Do I believe that I won't drown in my fears and phobias, but rise to the surface as gracefully as any paddleboarder?

Not sure. But at least I am asking myself the questions, big and fundamental questions of faith, as I gaze out across the miles, the thousands of miles that stretch before me between Rehoboth and Portugal, the water's surface rippled only by fish and sea birds. And as I stand at the edge, I pray for rest and renewal. But more, I pray that I can cast off in the boat of true discipleship, and to be a Peter, putting one foot in front of the other as the waves lap all around me. I pray that I can trust in the God who created me AND the ocean both, and will never let me sink.

As the sun sets over the bay, I cross off another precious day down here. I look forward to returning home soon, both recharged and changed. I hope you have found your own special places and times to be renewed this summer. And then, may we all reunite in September as the bold, daring, faith-filled people of God.

"I" IS FOR INDUCTION DAY

His hair had never been shaggier than it was that morning. His clothes were rumpled, and his eyes looked so tired. Of course, waking up at 4:00 AM will do that to an 18-year-old. As Evan would tell you, he didn't have to wake up quite that early. It was me who insisted, setting multiple alarms to make sure the whole family was up and at 'em well before dawn. After all, it was a two hour drive from our home to his institute of higher learning, and who knew what kind of traffic we would hit? Answer: we would hit NO traffic, not at 5:00 AM. We stopped for gas, then for coffee, and were still ridiculously early. But that was OK, because the instruction in his papers was clear. He was to report to the Naval Academy at 8:30 sharp, and one doesn't argue with such an official pronouncement. It was "I-Day", and Evan was about to be inducted into the US Navy.

We'd been to Annapolis before. Evan had been interested since freshman year of high school, so we had gone down and taken the tour. I remember trooping past the indoor pool with the group, and being informed that a jump from the 30 foot diving board was a prerequisite to graduation. My immediate reaction was horror (me, the queen of the kiddie pool). My son's reaction? "So cool!"

As he grew older and college decisions loomed, Evan was torn between a more conventional path and a military academy. Even after the acceptances began to come in, he remained conflicted. Finally, one night he emerged from his room and told us that he had decided to "sign his life away", as he put it with a laugh, and accept the offer from USNA.

But wait! This was our free spirit, our jazz pianist, the guy who liked to question just about everything, growing up. The least organized of our kids. Not exactly the portrait of the ideal midshipman. How would he fare with the orders, with the discipline? The shaggy-haired, weary boy who was shuffling along towards Alumni Hall did not give me great confidence in this pairing of school and student.

We stood with him on that warm late June morning, as the line of clearly nervous young people and their families grew longer by the minute. I could hear snippets of conversations…"Remember the day your brother started here?" "Three generations of Naval officers. You're keeping the tradition going, kiddo!" We had no such tradition, at least not on my side of the family. My dad's peak of achievement in the Army was peeling mountains of potatoes in a kitchen on a base in Florida during WWII. But my husband Steve's brother Phil was career Navy, so maybe that was the genetic connection. Still, I felt that we didn't really fit on this beautiful but intimidating campus, and that Evan might not either.

Suddenly there was no more time for doubts. Hurried hugs and he was gone, out of our sight. His head was shaved; he was given the supremely unattractive uniform of the "plebe". For the rest of the day, we remained on the grounds on our own. Evan was swept right into training, and given his copy of "the rates" (the rules) which he would need to start memorizing. From time to time, we saw knots of white-uniformed plebes being herded around by upperclassmen, who were shouting at them…not exactly a sight to bring joy to a mother's heart. We would see Evan again, briefly, at 6 PM, when he and his thousand fellow freshmen would gather in Tecumseh Court to take the Oath of Office.

I had always been able to pick Evan out in a crowd. Sometimes it was easy, like at the big fifth grade chorus concert when he was the only kid with a blue shirt on, in a sea of white shirts (I had missed the memo; Evan couldn't have cared less). Sometimes it was a bit more of a challenge. But that evening I scanned the throng and had absolutely no idea which one was my child. They all looked identical. And I wondered: would the Academy wipe out what made Evan, Evan? I prayed it would not, but I knew there were no guarantees.

Had I possessed that coveted (and, alas, nonexistent) parent's crystal ball and been able to look ahead ten years, past his four years as a midshipman, and six more as a Naval officer, I would have been very reassured. Evan remained fully himself (even down to playing jazz piano every chance he got). As for the changes—well, learning to clean a room well enough to pass an Alpha inspection was actually a GOOD thing. He was proud of his service, and grateful for the incredible education he received.

But that summer night in 2004, we left Annapolis with heavy hearts. We wouldn't see our son until the end of August, and meanwhile would only be able to get two three-minute phone calls from him. The experience of Plebe Summer would be Evan's, and not ours. As the beautiful, but intimidating, Naval Academy receded in our rear view mirror, we knew that it was "I-Day" for us as well, an induction into a whole different world, for Evan and for the family who loved him, that he was leaving behind.

BACK TO SCHOOL

It's back-to-school time! So many happy memories! Having a tug-of-war with another crazed mom in the aisle at Staples over the last 3" binder in the tri-state area! The chore of attempting (and attempting, and attempting) to waken my grouchy kids after a sleep-in summer! Filling out endless paperwork for all my little students the morning everything was due (I always hastily listed my nicest neighbor's information as our "emergency contact"—figuring I'd ask her permission later)!

Oh, wait. HAPPY memories?

Never mind.

Seriously, though, September always produces intense anxiety in me. As a child, I dreaded getting used to a new classroom, and a new teacher. I would have fared much better as a resident of the Little House on the Prairie, with the same predictable schoolmarm for eight straight years. Instead, as soon as I learned the ways of my fourth grade teacher, a sweet 19-year-old Irish nun named Sister Mary Brendan, it was time to acclimate myself to the stern and forbidding Miss Hibbard in fifth. Things never really improved, as I had to meet, then bid farewell to, a dizzying succession of instructors. Even in college, I would haunt the halls hoping to catch a glimpse of my really nice German teacher—while steering clear of my brilliant philosophy professor (I still have nightmares about the assignment:

"Discuss Anselm's ontological argument, then present your own proof of the existence of God." Hey, Anselm was a good guy! Why couldn't I just take his word for it?).

I work in a church, and our program year begins in September. While I no longer have to shop for school supplies, I do have to order Confirmation curriculum; I must beg and plead and call in favors to fill in my Sunday School teacher roster. I get very nostalgic for the way things used to be, when saintly Mr. and Mrs. Dome taught second grade Sunday School for over thirty years (my kids fondly remember the chocolate donuts they doled out each week; I fear they are less sharp on the Bible stories). But I know the culture has changed, churchgoing has declined all over, and to survive we need to be looking at new ways of doing spiritual formation. More anxiety!

But I do try to calm myself and count my blessings—no one in the house is applying to college this year, for example. Nobody is bringing home a "Friday folder" with the week's math tests and spelling papers for me to look over and sign either. I haven't packed a school lunch in years—no more running out of string cheese and peanut butter and that horrible yogurt you squeeze from a tube. No more time consuming and "clever" book report assignments. In third grade, the teacher fad was Book Report in a Can: empty aluminum cans that had to be covered with paper, then decorated with scenes from *The Indian in the Cupboard.* SO much work! And the kids even did a little bit of it too! My grandsons Aiden and Peter are too young for homework and gym uniforms, but not for long. All too soon my grandbabies will be boarding that big yellow school bus, but—and here's the difference—I won't be the one getting them ready! Good luck, Mom Ya-Jhu and Dad Sheridan!

Next week, when school is back in session, maybe I'll drive over to Jarrettown Elementary at dismissal and just sit in the car pool line for a while, for old times' sake. I may shed a tear as I remember my children, who used to clamber into the back seat, talking eagerly and breathlessly about what happened at recess. But after that, I will dry my eyes and give thanks that we all got through those crazy, exhausting years. And as I do, maybe I'll finally let go of my anxiety, which after all never did anyone any good, and learn at last to enjoy September.

Not going anywhere NEAR Staples, though.

TOO MUCH INFORMATION

The plots of lots of novels, movies and TV shows feature a man (or woman) of mystery, someone whose colorful, or tragic, or criminal past is shrouded in secrecy. Depending on the story, the mystery person either reveals all at the end, or someone else does the revealing. And the revealing usually takes quite some time.

Not like real life—especially real life today. Nowadays, the lifespan of a mystery is about five minutes, thanks to our friend the Internet. I know as much about Donald Trump's childhood as I do about my dad's (more, actually). I know a great deal more than I want to about Madonna's liaisons and Robert Downey Jr.'s stints in rehab. The entire juicy stories are just a click or quick Google search away, for the curious. And for the relatively incurious? They aren't spared the lowdown either, because the screaming headlines follow us everywhere—websites, newspapers, radio and TV.

We are in an age of too much—way too much—information. Your past is easily searchable by colleges and prospective employers (pics of your 16 year old self with a beer bottle in hand and all). And today's youth don't seem very concerned about that. They have become so used to chronicling their every party and concert that I truly don't think it dawns on them that some of those posts may not be wise. And frankly, nowadays, even if you try to hide your misdeeds, the world is one degree of separation away from finding out anyway.

And it isn't just the kids. Facebookers and Instagrammers of all ages post some amazingly intimate stuff about their lives—along with moment-by-moment reporting of their breakfasts, their exercise plans, the "lovable" antics of their children and pets. I confess that I have been guilty of this myself...will my toddler grandson Aiden thank me someday for that video of him running around wrapped in a bath towel? Cute, perhaps, but necessary to share? Not really.

As a writer, my subject matter is very often my own life, but my articles are carefully written, to reveal only what I am comfortable with folks knowing. It was my choice, for example, to write about my bipolar disorder diagnosis ten years ago. I have no intention of going into some other, sensitive areas of my life, and I certainly try hard to respect the privacy of my family and friends. But lots of my fellow writers seem to have no filter whatsoever, and gleefully dish ALL the dirt on themselves and everyone else.

God is, no matter how much we read, and study, and pray, still very much a mystery to us. We, who are so used to instant information, can get frustrated when, the more we "know", the less we understand. Does anyone truly "get" the Incarnation? The Resurrection? The creation of the universe(s)? Not me! Whenever I hear that someone has the Bible figured out, I run in the opposite direction, because what follows is usually wrong-headed (and often mean-spirited) guesswork. Life is full of hints and glimpses of the Divine, but never the whole picture.

I am delighted to notice that a great number of young people nowadays are fine with not "getting" all the mysteries of faith. They are comfortable with paradox and no easy answers. Why? Maybe it's BECAUSE the temporal world bombards them with too much information 24/7, that they don't need, or want, to have their spiritual lives all spelled out.

Someday I trust that we all will see face-to-face; for now, maybe it's OK to envision through that glass darkly. So I say: bring back the mystery! Some of it anyway! Let's give ourselves, and everyone else, a break, and a little privacy once in a while. Let's enjoy the wonderful mysteries of each other, our world, and our God.

CONFESSIONS OF A PREGNANT PETER PAN

"Honey, tell me honestly. Does this Peter Pan costume make me look pregnant?"

"Honestly? Don't turn sideways on stage."

It started innocently enough. Steve and I had been married for seven childless years. Our children's theatre was growing, and we finally felt financially sure-footed enough to try for a baby. The very first month, our efforts were rewarded by a positive pregnancy test. Hmmm. Maybe we weren't ready quite that quickly! But our joy and excitement overtook our hesitation, and we began figuring out our Grand Working Mom Plan.

At that time, the two of us were the sum total of "Family Stages". We wrote, directed and performed two-actor plays based on classic children's stories, and traveled to schools, libraries, summer camps and theatres across four states with our productions. We mostly loved our work, and our adorable young audiences (indeed, we credit these children with our desire to have some of our own). How tough would it be to ride out the first months as a mom-to-be in the spotlight?

Pretty tough, as it turned out. Morning sickness waits for no woman, so we had a bucket at the ready behind our backdrop, just in case. As a first-time preggo, I was terrified that any big theatrical move I made would immediately cause a miscarriage, so my inter-pretations of the swashbuckling "boy who wouldn't grow up" became very...tentative. No matter! We couldn't afford to hire another actor until I was at least six months along. So the families (the savvy par-ents, at least) embraced the willing suspension of disbelief as an in-creasingly hefty Cinderella danced (or rather, lumbered) around with her Prince Charming, as Dorothy clicked her ruby slippers together without actually being able to see those slippers over her big tummy.

When I stepped away late in my seventh month, and a terrific actress stepped right in, I was elated. I could do this working mom thing! Family Stages didn't need to miss a beat! I'd be back in the saddle just a few weeks after delivery! And sure enough, when baby Sheridan was just three weeks old, I was called to duty for a library show—and the saintly librarian held our squirming infant for the hour-long presentation. From then on, I performed most of the shows with a babysitter waiting in the wings. I would nurse the baby, then hand him off and take the stage.

This worked well enough for Baby #1.

I became pregnant with Evan 18 months later. At this point, I was "showing" earlier, so the costumes had to be let out (and I did heed the advice about facing forward at all times). Again, I made it within two months of delivery, took my little break, and returned. This time we required two sitters, one for toddler Sheridan and one for nursing baby Evan. As we peeled off the dollar bills at the end of the night, we added up what we were making to perform and realized the profitability gap was closing. But it was still worth it to soldier on, through productions of "Snow White" and "Alice in Wonderland" and "Pinocchio." I always got back in shape quickly—no exercise class needed when you spent your workday jumping and running and bouncing all over the set! At two, Sheridan could sit in the audience (though at times he would crow, "Hi Mommy!" which sort of broke the spell).

By the time Rose, Patrick and Julie joined the clan, I was in my mid to late thirties, a bit long in the tooth to play ingenues even if I hadn't been mere weeks post-partum. Luckily we were successful enough to hire young actors to take my place a lot of the time. And so my working days as a children's theatre performer dwindled to a precious few. I stayed heavily involved in other ways: booking shows, managing the box office, baking cookies for intermission. Even then, over time, Rosie took over the baking, and Julie became the Queen of the Box Office. Our teenage sons spent a few summers acting in our troupe in "Robin Hood" and "Puss in Boots." Family Stages remained largely that—a family affair. Until…

I was eventually offered a job at our church as spiritual formation director. The handwriting was on the wall. It was time for this working mom to quit doing this particular type of work. Our youngest, Julie, took it the hardest, as she loved my comic portrayals of Smee the Pirate and Miles the Town Crier. But eventually she, too, saw the wisdom of quitting while I was (somewhat) ahead.

Nowadays, we have a roster of actors working for our ever-increasing business. Steve keeps his hand in, playing the character roles (how old, after all, is too old to play Captain Hook?), but I have hung up my ruby slippers for good. I often think back on those frantic years, feeding a newborn just before my cue, squeezing into tights I had no business trying to wear, and honestly? I miss those crazy days, and sometimes I'd give anything to turn back the clock. But I am 60, and I can't do that.

So now, I sit in the audience instead, with my precious grandson Aiden. And as I say a final farewell to my working-actress-mother days, together, joyously, Aiden and I both clap and clap for Tinkerbell. And all is just as it should be.

QUEEN OF DENIAL

I live in a perpetual state of denial, about almost everything. Just one example: I haven't been to the dentist in (ahem) several years because I know my gums are receding. He will tell me that, and then I will have to do something about them, which will wind up being terribly painful both to mouth and pocketbook. Instead, I brush often but verrry gingerly, and try to smile in a way that does not betray a set of gums that is going out like the tide.

Similarly, I make a point of avoiding medical professionals in general. Whenever I accompany one of the kids to the doctor's, I don't touch any of the dog-eared issues of *Yachting World* and *Highlights for Children* lying around the waiting room. I just know they have recently been handled by sick people, such as the guy three chairs over who has been coughing up a lung for 15 minutes. Of course, I wouldn't dream of getting a flu shot, but I somehow feel that keeping my hands off the *People* magazines will preserve my health.

I deny the irrefutable fact that I have regained the 25 pounds I lost when I started taking the antidepressant Wellbutrin nine years ago. Those size zero dresses and pants still occupy much of my closet, because I refuse to believe that I will never (ever) weigh 105 pounds again. I deny that I am getting older by dyeing my hair (that'll fool 'em!) and, in lieu of pricey anti-aging creams, I just look in the mirror without wearing my eyeglasses, which immediately erases my wrinkles. By the way, for many years I denied that my vision was getting worse, and even now, the specs remain in their case for the most part. I compensate for that by getting rides to my every nighttime destination if at all possible. When I do this, I feel like a 90-year-old, but at least the roads are safer without me squinting and swerving down the highways and byways.

I hate winter weather (which makes Philadelphia of course a choice place of residence). I therefore wear shorts and flip flops until the first snowfall, willing the temperature to climb back into the Swell 70s again. This crazy meteorological year, I have actually been dressed appropriately in my summery duds, even in December. Normally, though, this denial of the arctic chill has been known to make me ill. And when I do get sick, I never take any cold remedies, even as my nose runs like the proverbial faucet. "I'm fine!" I insist, through miserable sore throats and raging fevers. "Just—achoo!—fine!"

Around the house, I refused to believe there was anything wrong with the refrigerator until the meat in there almost started to cook. I didn't admit that the chimney was in desperate need of repair until bricks began falling into the yard. When company comes, I light every candle in the house, and don't let myself think about the dust bunnies that would surely be revealed with the flip of a switch.

At work, my computer is definitely in its dotage. Every time I turn it on, I can almost hear it creaking and moaning, so it's only a matter of time before I boot up and see the dreaded "blue screen of death" (the sure sign that the computer has crashed). But while I know my PC will go kaput any day now, I stubbornly refuse to back up my files. At risk are months and months of church work, as well as freelance articles, photos, etc. Like a really bad gambler, I am betting that all will magically be preserved with no effort on my part. Looking around my office, I pretend the teetering stacks of books and CDs make me look "busy and productive". If I allowed myself to feel shame about the immense amount of clutter on and around my desk, I might have to clean up, and we can't have that!

In short, I deny more things than an accused criminal on the witness stand. Reality, as the saying goes, bites. So why face it until you absolutely have to? Mine is a dream world where gums heal themselves, fallen bricks hop back onto chimneys, and laptops never break. You're welcome to join me!

FITBIT TO BE TIED

Dear Fitbit,

I'm not sure quite how to put this. I really don't want to hurt you. But I think we need to take a break.

I know, we haven't been together long, but your degree of clinginess has been suffocating me. You literally never let go of my wrist, and every time I get an email or a text you have to buzz like crazy and let me know. Well, guess what? I can check my own messages without being treated like Pavlov's dog.

And here's another thing. You're always judging judging judging. Sure, you give a little virtual cheer when I reach my daily goal, but I can tell you're just being sarcastic. So what if I set my goal as 100 steps a day? It's doable! Which is more than I can say about that ridiculous 10,000 steps goal that everybody else in the world seems to have! I can't tell you how weird it is to be chatting with a friend late at night and have them suddenly get up and pace, because it's 11:45 PM and they're only at 9,000 steps. I ask you, and I ask you this sincerely, who the heck cares?

There are lots of other facets to you, bells and whistles like totaling up my mileage, and even asking me about my sleep. What business is that of yours? The way I see it, unless I am sleepwalking, there is nothing about my nocturnal habits that should concern you. Let me have my space, for Heaven's sake!

I have tried taking you off in the shower, at the beach, leaving you on my bedside table. But still you bug me, with regular email notifications about reaching (or more likely NOT reaching) my weekly goals. Sometimes I just want to do something drastic, like package you up and return you to Amazon, but something tells me you'd still find a way to keep in contact. Worse, you might start sharing the intimate details of my daily slothfulness with your next owner! "Congratulations! You have reached your goal of 50,000 steps today! Elise Seyfried, on the other hand, has yet to break 50! Don't be like Elise Seyfried!"

I realize that the simplest solution is to just let you wind down and not recharge you, but for some reason that feels like cheating to me. I need to be brave and face you, woman to piece of rubber with a battery in it, and tell you how I feel. So here goes: I feel guilty, 24/7, when I'm with you. Every time I sit down (which is admittedly most of the time), I am acutely aware that I "should" be up and moving. Listen, sweetheart, I am already plenty guilty about my eating habits and my sloppy housecleaning! I don't need to get depressed for just taking a load off my feet!

So let's just agree to put a little distance (say, 10,000 steps) between us for a while. You can chill in a drawer, and I can live my slower paced life without constant reminders that I should be doing better. What say I stop and smell the roses, and maybe you can relax too. I will gladly store you right next to my Jack Johnson CDs, and hopefully you can catch that vibe. I swear it will do you good.

For now, let's say goodbye. Now now, Fitbit, don't cry! It's not you, really. It's me.

Love, Elise

MAI PEN RAI

Mai pen rai: whatever, it's all good, it's fine. You say it when someone asks if you mind watching their choice of TV show, or if someone steps on your toes. Thais are unfailingly polite. Mai pen rai is a gentle phrase that keeps things pleasant, no matter what. It is a different way of looking at the world, which makes sense, as Thailand is exactly halfway around the globe. It is also the way our teenage daughter learned to see things when she lived there.

The adventure began the day after Christmas of 2004. High school sophomore Maureen Rose had made it through the interview process, and been accepted as a Rotary International exchange student. The tradition was that the students would select their top ten choices of countries to live in, and at a special dinner their assigned locations would be revealed. I remember her joy when she opened her envelope and read "Thailand," as countries in Asia were definitely her top choices. After dinner, I called my sister, and only then did I hear about the devastating tsunami that had just hit the country that day. "You aren't letting her go THERE?" Carolyn asked worriedly. Actually, yes, we were. She wouldn't leave until the following summer, and then would be going to a city in the mountainous region of northern Thailand, hundreds of miles from the ocean.

And so, at age 16, Maureen left home to live for a year in Chiang Rai, Thailand. She was one of 3,000 students at Damrongsonkroh

High School, and one of the few falangs (foreigners) there. She left in 2005, when Skype was in its early stages and there were no such things as iPhones. As our family gathered at the airport to see her off, there were many tears shed, because we knew communication going forward would be difficult. Mo was flying to Bangkok via Detroit (where she would meet up with other Rotary students). Our oldest, Sheridan, broke the somber mood when he yelled after her: "Mo! Have a good time in Detroit!" and the other passengers shook their heads in wonder at the family who couldn't stop crying when sending their child to Michigan.

Aside from a hasty "I survived" call when she landed, we heard nothing more for a couple of weeks. Then came the emails, typed on her host parents' computer in their modest house. At first, she talked about her sense of loneliness: her host brother and sister had left home, and their parents worked insane hours, so Mo was often alone at the house, with servants who delivered her meals. But she also gave us marvelous glimpses of the rich and exotic culture she had entered, and it was clear to us that, most of the time, she was more happy than homesick.

Soon she made friends, girls with names like Book and Fa, and boys who breakdanced in the square in the evenings. She took classes in Thai flower arranging, dance and fruit-carving. She pushed to be part of the school military training, rawdaw, one of the only girls to do so. She traveled all over the country, even eventually to Phuket on the coast, where the tsunami had done the most damage. There she heard heartbreaking stories from the hotel workers about loved ones and homes lost.

By spring, she was conversant in Thai, well on her way to fluency. The written language with its completely different alphabet was starting make sense. She asked for hacky sacks from home, and taught her friends to play with the colorful knitted balls. She amassed a wardrobe of beautiful clothing items that cost just a few dollars (baht) each, and became a big fan of Thai pop music. She loved it when people referred to her as "half-Thai," because I'm sure that's how she felt. At some point, she got her tongue pierced (at the Thai equivalent of K-Mart—so glad I didn't know about this till she got home!). And, at some point, she changed her name.

She was born Maureen Rose, and had always gone by her first name, Maureen. In Chiang Rai, she embraced her middle name (Rose) for good. As symbolic as a bride taking a new last name, our daughter had reinvented herself in the land of sweet smiles, strange foods, and gorgeous scenery. It was like saying goodbye to Mo forever, and meeting a brand-new person—Rose, a confident young woman who rode on the back of motorcycles and bargained at night markets. Who played takraw (kind of a kickball-volleyball hybrid) with her classmates, and ate tiny jumping bugs from a bamboo steamer. Who had let go of much of her anxiety and stress, and said "mai pen rai" when tricky situations arose.

She's been home for years, and I'm sure some of her memories are fading. Amazingly, she still understands and speaks some Thai (she is a big hit ordering at Thai restaurants). She still keeps in touch with some of her good friends from Chiang Rai. And she is still Rose, who left us as an American teenager, and came home as a citizen of the world. Rose has a wonderful but stressful job in New York City now, and I hope she taps into the gentle, loving and easygoing spirit of her Thai brothers and sisters when she needs it. Worried? Troubled? It's all good. Mai pen rai.

A RESURRECTION REFLECTION

Steve and I were out for our anniversary dinner last night, and driving down our street we noticed that many of our neighbors had their trash cans out, in anticipation of our Friday morning collection. We remarked that this weekly ritual seemed to be happening every couple of days, as our lives have definitely picked up their pace. This is rather a shame. The years I would l have loved to fast-forward through (can you say "middle school"?) crept by, and now that I am aging I would appreciate a little creeping by, instead of my sped-up reality.

I know this is all merely perception—time is moving at exactly the same rate as it always has. Perhaps I am just ever more aware of the brevity of even the longest life. This past week, several members of our congregation died, and a number of funerals are taking place. A few of these dear folks were in their late 90s, a "ripe old age" indeed, but I know their families and friends will still miss them terribly, and their lives will be forever different without them. Every passing changes the world a little bit.

And so does every birth. This same week, the Kelly family welcomed their third child, a baby girl. If little Audra lives until HER late 90s we are looking at the 2100s, a date that sounds just as science-fictiony as 1984 used to, or 2001. For perspective, if I am still kicking around at that point I will be pushing 150, a positively Old Testament length of years. Kinda doubt it!

Life on earth, for all of us, is bookmarked by our birth and our death. We have no control over the date of either—we could just as well have been born during the American Revolution, or died during the Renaissance. The fact that we are here, co-existing on this planet in 2018, is pretty random, right?

I would say "wrong." I believe that it is NOT mere chance that put me here, now. The God who made me and loves me, knew I would be living in 21st century Oreland when I was 61. I am part of God's plan for humanity, and it is up to me to make this time count, in many ways. I need to be a loving wife to Steve and mom to my kids and Nana to Aiden and Peter. But I need to spread even more love around, to my friends, my church family, and the world at large. In my words and actions, I need to advocate for peace and justice. I need to live with intention and awareness, no matter how accelerated the pace of my precious days.

As Christians, we have faith in Christ's resurrection promise to us: that we will continue to exist after taking our last earthly breath. That we will reunite with our loved ones who passed before us, and that we will in turn welcome those arriving in Heaven after us. I think of eternity with joy and anticipation, and I thank God we all have that to look forward to. When the worries and fears of our world begin to overwhelm me, I can think of Easter and be comforted and reassured.

We are quickly (very quickly) approaching Easter 2018. I pray for the families of those recently deceased; I pray for the families of the new babies too. Wherever we are on our journeys, let us pause and reflect on our immortality, the great gift of God's love for us. As we see the daffodils and crocuses pushing upward through the snow, so will we have new life after our winter. It's a blessing. It's a miracle. Union with Pure Love, forever.

Meanwhile, let's take out our trash cans every Thursday night, and try to live our best lives between those mundane weekly chores. Because we are, newborn and centenarian alike, God's precious ones, and we have a great destiny. Let's savor every step of our way home.

THE SEYF-ELISE
METHOD OF CLEANING

I recently read Japanese super-organizer Marie Kondo's bestseller *The Life-Changing Magic of Tidying Up* and boy! Let me tell you, I am motivated! She got me at "life-changing magic" (not so much the tidying up part, but still…). I've decided that it's time to take control of my possessions. Kondo walks the reader through the various steps of sorting, discarding, etc. My scattered brain can't begin keep these steps in order, so I kinda skipped around, "sorting" her advice and "discarding" anything I didn't feel like doing. In the process, I learned an inconvenient truth or two about myself, but by and large it was a GREAT experience. Let's plunge right in, shall we?

Marie Kondo (or Kon-Mari as she is known to her legion of fans) describes herself as a neatnik and demon organizer from the cradle, spending school recess time straightening her entire classroom, spending her allowance on home decorating magazines. Here's where we part company right away. My desk at school overflowed with garbage, from used-up pencils to wads of gum wrapped in tissues. Oh, I did my homework assignments—I just could never find them. My allowance was spent primarily on the Columbia Record Club. The fabulous introductory offer of 12 LPs for $1 was what sucked me in, but then came the monthly nightmare of forgetting to cancel shipments and paying ridiculous bills for *The Best of The Partridge Family*. By the time I finally extricated myself, I could have opened a (very large) record store.

Kon-Mari suggests we begin by gathering all of one type of item in one place...clothes, books, etc. We are to touch one thing at a time, and ask ourselves if it brings us joy. Hold it right there! "Things" don't bring me joy—relationships do! Nature does! Travel does! Experiences! Soooo...out it all goes, right? Not so fast! I have a very complicated relationship with my stuff. How else to explain my spatula collection (at least 12, and I don't recall buying any of them)? Or my array of decorative cheese spreaders? These fall into the category of "semper paratus"—always ready. Pancake flipping contest? Wheel of Brie rolling up to my doorstep? I'm good to go! Joy is beside the point!

Kondo urges me to reduce the items in my possession until something "clicks"—the sublime moment when I know, in my heart, that I have enough. But what, I wonder, does that "click" sound like? Is it the same "click" I don't hear when I need to decide about that third cream-filled donut? Because if it is, I am definitely click-impaired. She also—and this is where it gets strange—wants me to ask myself if my clothes would be "happier" hung up or folded.

This is the same woman who thanks her belongings for their service to her before she passes them along, who audibly greets her home upon her evening return. Come on, Marie—aren't human-to-human interactions stressful enough? I can't be the only person to have been trapped in an endless loop of deadly conversation with a cashier: "Thank you!" "Thank YOU!" "Have a nice day!" "You have a GREAT day!" "You too!" "Stay warm (or cool, depending on the season)!" "You too!" aaaannddd we're back to "thank you!" I honestly want my belongings to keep their mouths shut and stop being so darned opinionated. "Silence is golden," I tell my sweaters. And I will greet my house when my house shows me that an effort has been made in my absence. Even the dishwasher unloading itself would count. Vacuuming would be awesome as well.

The heart of the book can be summed up thusly: "What you want to own is how you want to live your life." See, that's the thing. I don't WANT to own anything, it just happens. Ditto my life. So here we are. And as I lug my megaton of things with me through my days, I know it's finally time to make some choices. So what'll it be? 12 spatulas? Or...10?

Why don't we start with something easier?

UP IN SMOKE

My dad smoked four packs a day. Those cigs were in his mouth from dawn until late evening. Every morning, my childhood chore was to empty the brimming ashtrays after they cooled overnight. As a teenager, I wanted so badly to have a good relationship with this quiet, detached father of mine—so, of course, I tried smoking too. As I choked on my Virginia Slims, I imagined (a pipe dream, if you will) the two of us sitting on the porch after dinner, chatting companionably about—well, I never got past that point in my reverie. But cigarettes were always involved, and lots of them.

Not surprisingly, Dad had a massive stroke at age 67. His last conscious act was holding a cigarette and a lighter, and then just staring at his hands, unable to figure out what to do next. By then I was married with four kids and one on the way, and lived 1000 miles from my parents. But I flew down right away, sat at his bedside in the hospital during the last week of his life, and slept every night in their apartment, which reeked of tobacco. My first trimester stomach rebelled at the stench, but it was important to be with my mom as much as possible.

Dad had indicated an interest in cremation, not seeing the irony at all. We passed that wish along to the funeral director, and my dad was quickly turned into more ashes in a tray. Then I went to my folks' Catholic church to plan the memorial service. To my dismay, I learned that my cremated father could not come into the church for the Catholic funeral, as his body had not been properly blessed and embalmed first. So my father, for years the church's head usher, had to settle for a blessing at home from a kind priest friend. Then Dad was placed gently on a shelf. What next? Where and when to scatter? Dad had seemed to enjoy the seashore, so we made a plan to rent a boat and go out into the Delaware Bay that summer.

It was a very windy day out on the water. The waves were choppy, and my husband struggled to drive the boat. While our other kids expressed no interest in being part of this ritual, for some reason eight-year-old Evan asked if he could go with us. The three of us (four, counting Dad) hung on as the little vessel dipped and swayed. Suddenly, all was still. It seemed like a sign from Heaven that this was our moment. Hastily I said a few sentimental words, and opened the box. Immediately the wind picked up again, and the ashes blew all over, many landing on Evan, who thankfully didn't seem to notice. I dumped the remainder overboard and we headed back to the marina, Evan looking just like a miniature chimney sweep.

Dad is gone 23 years now. I never did become a smoker, and Steve only smokes the very occasional cigar while playing poker. Losing my father so early, and from such an avoidable cause, has certainly had a great impact on my life. I can't stand to be around people who are puffing away. I still wonder if my health has been compromised by the massive amount of secondhand smoke I grew up with. And my parenting has been impacted as well.

Julie, who was born seven months after Dad died, still mourns the loss of the grandfather she never met. The older ones have only the dimmest recollections of him. My kids have been told many times that, had it not been for those four packs a day, they might have had Grandpa for many more years. I hoped that reminder would be enough to keep them all smoke-free, and for the most part it has.

So much time has passed. Dad and I never did develop the close relationship I had yearned for all those years ago. I can go for weeks now without thinking of him. But every once in a while, on the street, I pass a group of smokers huddled outside an office building. I catch a whiff of burning tobacco, the signature scent of my childhood, and suddenly, I remember.

LITTLE CAVE OF WONDERS

Bet you didn't know that we have a cave in our family room! Lucky us, right? Actually, Aiden is the cave dweller, and his imaginative abode is a small area in the family room behind the rocking chair. He can barely move back there, squeezed as he is between the chair and a side table, but no matter! It's his hideaway! The entrance to the cave is his plastic Lego case, which is empty and thus very prone to falling over. I have mentioned this structural flaw to him, but he will have no other "door". Which would be well and good were he an only child, but he has a baby brother (I almost typed "baby bother", which now that I think of it also fits). Peter adores Aiden, and shows it by his persistence in trying to enter the Little Cave of Wonders. As the Lego case goes crashing down yet again, we hear, "Nooooooooo! Peter!! This is not your cave!! Go away, Peter!!!!"

Ever since young Peter began to crawl (and climb!), Aiden has felt besieged. He has taken to carrying his most prized toys around in his pockets for safekeeping. As I had with my own kids, I tell him that it will get better, that soon the two of them will be boon companions. Aiden always looks at me as if I had two heads. I know just what he's thinking: *Play? With him? I don't THINK so!*

But the other night, we had a playtime breakthrough of sorts. Peter, a recent walker, enjoys carrying an empty milk jug around with him on his staggers through the house. Inspiration struck, and we started inviting Peter to bring Aiden some "strawberry milk". Almost immediately, the little guy caught on, lugging the jug over and pretending to pour the contents into Aiden's cupped hands. He repeated his popular performance again and again. Whew! Peace and harmony! But wait! Within five minutes, Peter had sent the Lego case door toppling over, and small brother was again persona non grata.

Aiden's cave and Peter's empty milk jug remind me that the very best plaything is the imagination. Some of my happiest childhood memories involved lying in bed at night and pretending the ceiling was the floor, or finding faces in the knotty-pine paneling at the summer cottage. While, as a young mom, I did my darnedest to replicate Toys R Us in our home, I noticed that it was the open-ended play items (blocks, play-doh) that proved by far the most popular.

Wise Yaj and Sheridan do not overwhelm their children with stuff, and as a result they love what they have. I remember our "corn popper" push toy gathering dust, ignored by my offspring. The exact same toy is still on the market, and Aiden has played with it every day for two years, taking it with him down the street to the park, using it as a lawn mower in the yard. Peter also adores the corn popper on the rare occasions that he is allowed to touch it (it is usually kept inside Aiden's cave).

All too soon the family room will revert to just a bunch of furniture in one place. The kids will move on, and the magic cave will recede into the past. But I hope they never forget Aiden's crazy Lego case door, and Peter's gift of strawberry milk, and the simple joys of play. I know I never will.

YA-JHU AND THE JADE BANGLE

We've been mother-and-daughter-in-law for five years now, and I've never found the right gift for her. Sometimes I ask her husband, my son Sheridan. That's usually not helpful, because Sheridan is totally uninterested in "things". Asking him about Ya-Jhu's preferences elicits a sigh, and then: "I don't think she needs anything, Mom. So anything you give her would be fine." So I take a guess, and give her a sweater, or a scarf. She is always very gracious, but deep down I feel I've missed the mark. This year would be no exception, I feared. And with two little ones now, two-year-old Aiden and infant Peter, my daughter-in-law really deserved a thoughtful present from me.

Yaj came to the United States from her home in Taiwan, pursuing graduate degrees in music composition from the Manhattan School of Music in New York, and, later, the Curtis Institute in Philadelphia. She came alone, traveling without family or friends. Within a few years, she had several commissioned works performed, she got that Master's and that Curtis diploma, and she had stolen the heart of a young American composition student who happened to be my firstborn. Soon they were engaged, then married. And then the babies began to arrive.

Her parents traveled to Philadelphia for the wedding, but haven't made it back since. With Ya-Jhu's mom 10,000 miles away, I've had to stand in many times—when she was in labor, when she needed quick mothering advice. Skyping with Taipei only goes so far. I cannot communicate with my counterpart at all. She speaks no English, and the extent of my Chinese is: "ni hao" (hello), "haochi" (tasty), and "diannao" (computer)—not exactly the perfect words for a meaningful conversation between mothers-in-law.

During the summer, Yaj and I were together down at the shore in Lewes, Delaware. One afternoon we wandered into an antique store that had a display case of heirloom jewelry. I am the world's most unobservant person, but for some reason I noticed Ya-Jhu staring at a beautiful green jade bangle in the case. For months afterward I thought about that bracelet, and regretted not buying it and setting it aside. I resigned myself to picking out yet another sweater or scarf, for which she would profusely thank me—but we'd both know it wasn't a perfect fit.

One night, I couldn't sleep, and found myself on the internet looking for jade bangles. Lo and behold, I found a lovely one, so I ordered it immediately. I hoped she still liked jade. I hoped she wouldn't be secretly disappointed. And then I waited.

When she opened the package, she cried, "Mom! How did you know? This is a traditional gift from mothers to daughters in Taiwan!" I was flabbergasted. It had never crossed my mind that the jade bangle might have any significance beyond being a pretty piece of jewelry. My daughter-in-law slid it over her tiny left wrist. For once, I had scored as a gift giver!

The next day, I read more about the present I had given Ya-Jhu. In Chinese culture, jade is very special. It is said to ward off bad fortune. A jade bracelet is worn on the left wrist, and some wearers never take it off. Sure enough, mothers give them to their daughters as symbols of their love and protection. Totally unwittingly, I had given Yaj something that was very meaningful in her homeland. More than that, I had given her a gift that meant she was really a daughter to me, which was nothing but the truth.

In the years to come, I doubt my gifting skills will improve much, and I don't hold out any higher hope for my ability to speak Mandarin. It will still be a challenge to connect with my new extended family in Taiwan with the few words I will manage to remember. But when I look at Ya-Jhu, I will see the treasured jade bracelet on her arm, an accidental symbol of our abiding love, and I will be content.

MAP QUEST

It's a game they played back in January. Every night Evan left a voice-mail message, telling his nephew Aiden where he had stopped for the night. Aiden then went downstairs to the big United States map on the wall, found the destination (with a little help) and put a push pin there. His shushu (Chinese for "uncle") covered a lot of territory during his week of traveling west. Evan needed to be in California to start his new job as finance director for a congressional campaign, a move which involved many, many miles on the road. Evan's luck held, and he did not run into terrible winter driving conditions (he deliberately plotted a more southerly course). Aiden believed Evan would make it to Orange County on time, and he did.

Aiden has always loved maps of all kinds. He is also crazy about Evan Shushu. That combination has been a winner, because Evan has traveled quite a bit during Aiden's four years, and my little grandson loves to trace his adventures. Sometimes the journeys have been American, such as Ev's cross-country drive helping a friend resettle on the West Coast. Other times, Aiden has needed to switch over to the world map on the other side of the room, where even at a very young age he could point out Barcelona (where Evan went to graduate school) and other spots Evan hit in Europe and Asia. Last year, his intrepid uncle went with another buddy to Argentina for five weeks of trekking that included time down in Patagonia. This location particularly fascinated Aiden for some unknown reason. Several times daily, Aiden would put on his small backpack and head for the front door. "I'm goin' to see Shushu in Argentina!!" he would call out. We would solemnly wish him safe travels. Three minutes later he would zip back into the room, journey completed.

What, I wonder, does Aiden think of all these places, depicted in so many different colors and shapes on his maps? He can locate many of them, and knows some personal connections attached to them too: Indiana, where Steve was born; New York City, where I was born; Thailand, where Rose Gugu ("aunt") spent a year. Aiden himself has been to Taiwan three times, and can easily zero in on Taipei, where mom Ya-Jhu's family lives.

When I was a little girl, I pictured the world as incredibly diverse and exciting. I, too, pored over multicolored maps, imagining myself on safari in Tanzania, at a beach on Maui, climbing the Eiffel Tower. Then I grew up. I spent time in many different US cities, and was sadly struck by the sameness of so much that I saw—identical fast food restaurants, malls, hotel chains. Endless stretches of interstate, with green and white signs that only differed in the names of the exits. It was so disappointing! Had the world become like a giant theme park, with everything predictable and replicable?

However, in recent years, looking past the surface, and especially meeting a great many people, I am heartened to realize that little me was right—every place IS special and unique. Though McDonald's is certainly ubiquitous, and American entertainment (for better and worse) has reached around the globe, there are sharp distinctions between the gulf coast of Alabama and the mountains of West Virginia, different topography and accents and attitudes. Our greatest challenge—coming to understand each other and appreciate what we each have to offer—can also be our greatest strength.

I am so grateful that my loved ones and I have been able to travel, and I look forward to Aiden experiencing the wide world as much more than push pins in a map. Putting on a big backpack someday, walking out of the house, and really meeting his beloved shushu in the amazing Argentina of his dreams.

MY MUG RUNNETH OVER

It looks rather nondescript to the casual observer. It holds hot coffee. It has a handle. What's the big deal? Answer: it is by far my favorite mug, and it's a miracle that it's still on duty.

You see, I have a tendency to break things. I have broken countless glasses over the years, and more than a few plates. This is because I am a clumsy and totally disinterested dish washer. I also break necklaces and lose earrings regularly, because I am a slapdash and indifferent jewelry wearer. In short, you should not trust me with any delicate item you own (I know I certainly don't!).

And what I don't break, I lose. "Oh, it'll turn up!" I say to myself when I am missing my car key, when my favorite mixing bowl disappears, when I am down to one glove. Inevitably, "it" (whatever it is) is never seen again. I'm sure my sister Carolyn regrets that I was the one who ended up with our Nana's china statues of characters from Gilbert and Sullivan's *The Mikado*. Nana taught music and often staged operettas with her New York City students. The figurines were a treasured retirement gift from them. As of today, I have only one little statue left, and one of the arms has broken off.

On the other hand, there have been several items in my life I have wished <u>would</u> break or be lost, so that I could replace them with better-quality merchandise—yet those are the things that remain with me, no matter what. Hard to justify a new fridge when Old Faithful still chugs along, with its dented exterior, tilted shelves and ice maker that only works when it darn well feels like it. But it keeps the food cold, so technically it still "works". Ditto my 1980's chic mauve bedside table lamps—yes, they are really ugly. But yes, they still light up, so I guess there's no urgent need to replace them.

So how is it that I still have my very favorite coffee mug, which I received from Steve on my first Mother's Day, almost 33 years ago? Not only do I still have it, but it has nary a chip, and the design on the mug is as colorful as it was on Day One (even after countless trips through the dishwasher). It has never once gone missing. It is my mug of choice for my four daily huge doses of caffeine. Whenever I was pregnant and off the java, my "mom" mug was filled with hot cocoa instead. I always thought I had broken the coffee habit at last—until right after each delivery. I'd ask for coffee almost before I'd ask to hold the baby! It is probably my imagination, but I maintain my brewed Starbucks "bold" blend tastes even bolder when poured into my magic mug.

When our grandson Aiden came along, he was enthralled by my mug. The design (the word MOM spelled out in many different sizes and colors) is an eye-catcher, and a great way to practice an early word. Aiden used to have breakfast sitting on my lap, and would point gleefully to each MOM, vocalizing every one ("Momomomomomomom!"). So now, when I sip my hot beverages, I savor happy memories of my little guy too.

I know it's just a thing, and one of these days it is bound to finally break or be lost. But after 33 years it holds the record for longest-used item in the house, and I hate to think of the day when it will be no more. Oh, I have a cabinet filled with other mugs, souvenirs of trips to Jamaica and Guatemala. A mug from Patrick's college semester in Germany. A mug from Think Coffee in Manhattan, where Julie is a barista. I would be sorry to wave goodbye to any of them. But the "mom" mug has a special place in my heart. It has survived over three decades with me, and that is no small feat. Protecting it requires me to handle it with care, and that is very good for me.

My mug is at my side as I write this. The cheery red and blue and green lettering reminds me that I AM a "mom", five times over, a fact which, even after all these years, still amazes me. And while I know I define myself in other ways too, my favorite role in life is right there, and I hope it always will be. Printed on an ordinary, extraordinary coffee mug.

THE HAUNTING OF ROSS CASTLE

When the girls and I were planning our trip to Ireland last June, Rose and Julie's special request was to find a haunted castle to sleep in. Don't know how much they actually believe, but they are two gutsy gals; to them, it just sounded like fun. There are quite a few supposedly haunted castles in Ireland—and many brave tourists who seek them out. We settled on Ross Castle, in Montnugent.

Picture your stereotypical 14th century Irish stone castle, set majestically on a hill by a lake (Loch Sheelin), and you're picturing Ross Castle. We were given the choice of staying on the ground level (which included the grand dining hall and several bedrooms), or up a winding staircase in the tower. I selected the ground floor, because a) it seemed more comfortable, and b) if there WERE ghosts, wouldn't they be hanging out in the tower? That way I'd get credit for sleeping in proximity to spirits, without being threatened by their actual appearance. My girls were a little bummed I think, but went along with the plan.

Our hosts, Jackie and Richard Moeran, told us that Ross was a famously haunted castle. They were often visited by folks who set up their cameras and recording devices in the tower, hoping for a close encounter of the spooky kind. According to Richard, several visitors had seen the ghost over the years. We then heard the romantic and tragic tale of Sabina Nugent and Orwin O'Reilly. Sabina was the daughter of the baron whose noble Anglo-Norman family owned the castle, many hundreds of years ago. Orwin was a commoner, and Celtic-Irish. Naturally, their love could never be, which of course didn't stop them from falling in love anyway. One moonlit night, the pair was crossing Loch Sheelin, and the boat capsized. Orwin drowned; Sabina survived. A few weeks later, Sabina herself died, of a broken heart.

The Ross Castle ghost is Sabina, who roams the upper story of the castle looking for her lost Orwin. The Moerans are completely at peace with Sabina's co-habitation. They have had furniture moved around and heard strange noises over the years, but believe her to be quite harmless. That first night, we slept moderately well. Rose and Jules were hoping to see or hear Sabina; I was hoping not to. Aside from an odd sounding laugh I heard around 3 AM (most likely a dream), it was an uneventful night.

The following evening, our last in the castle, we were informed that there were no other guests booked, and that they (Richard and Jackie) would be sleeping in their house on the property. "You'll be fine!" Jackie chirped. "I'll be back in time to make breakfast!" On our own now, the castle suddenly took on a certain creepiness we hadn't noticed before. We sat in the common area with books, but didn't turn the pages. Too quiet. Then we decided to pull out Julie's laptop and watch something. Something funny. We were laughing away at some comedy special, and I began to relax. At that moment, we heard a key turn, and the front door swung open.

We looked at each other in horror. No other guests! Who could it be? Maybe Sabina had decided to enter the castle as a living human would for a change, instead of floating through a wall! We sat, paralyzed with fear. Suddenly, rounding the corner into the room…

…were two definitely mortal sisters from Finland. Jackie had forgotten they were booked, and gave them the key at her house when they arrived. The chatty young ladies informed us that they looked forward to sleeping in the tower, because they wanted very much to see Sabina. Their house in Finland was also haunted, and they were very accustomed to living with apparitions. Their ghost was also friendly, only doing a bit of furniture moving from time to time. (What is it with ghosts and moving furniture? Are they all interior designers or something?) The girls hoisted their suitcases and said good night, heading for the stone staircase and their hoped-for rendezvous with the spirit world.

We slept very well that night, sure that Sabina, if she was around, was busy entertaining our Nordic pals. When morning came, our fellow castle-dwellers joined us for breakfast. They were quite disappointed: Sabina Nugent had been a no-show. As we drove away down the winding gravel driveway, the Seyfried ladies were a little sad, but for different reasons. For me, it was the realization that our wonderful time in Ireland was coming to an end. For Rose and Julie, it was knowing that they had missed their chance to meet the Ghost of Ross Castle.

Back in the states now, I remain pretty skeptical about tales of the supernatural. I'm home in Oreland, and it's impossible to imagine anything paranormal in this most profoundly normal of suburbs. I'm just as glad to draw a curtain once more between this world and the next. Someday, we'll all know if we can return to earth to visit the places and people we loved. When that day comes, and if I become a ghost, I will not waste my time rearranging sofas, I can tell you that. I will pop in on my family and friends when they least expect it. I'll moan, groan, turn lights off and on, and scare them all silly. I figure, if you only live more than once, and you're gonna haunt—well then, haunt!

STORY SLAMMED

You know the old saying, "Always the bridesmaid, never the bride"? Well, I was reminded of that Friday night downtown, as once again I was <u>not</u> chosen to tell a story at a story slam. Now, mind you, that was only the second slam I had put my name in a hat for, but at this point I get it: I will NOT be picked. Ever.

For the uninitiated, a story slam is a performance featuring storytellers, chosen randomly from the audience, who have five minutes each to knock everyone's socks off in quest of a cash prize. You must come prepared to perform, then wait to be selected (or not). Watching a slam is fun; waiting to be chosen, not so much.

My first foray into slamdom happened about two years ago, with a story slam at the World Café in West Philly. I foolishly thought I had a chance, and toted several friends down with me. Rose even surprised me and came all the way from New York. I had a great tale to tell, and I was more than ready to tell it! We wannabe storytellers were instructed to fill out a paper with our names, which would then be placed in a hat. From that hat would be drawn the performers for the evening. I recall sitting, nervous but excited, awaiting my turn at the mic. I planned to relate the story of my ill-fated filming of a low-budget local TV commercial in Knoxville, Tennessee, many moons ago. It had everything! Humor! Suspense! Absurdity! It was a commercial for Kay's Ice Cream, filmed by the producer's hapless son in his mother's kitchen. The comedy of errors included industrial lights burning the kitchen ceiling, and an un-plugged freezer containing the star of the show (melted vanilla, anyone?).

Every time the emcee's hand fished in the hat for the name of the next storyteller, I started to stand up, much like those over-eager awards show nominees. But alas! The name "Seyfried" never escaped his lips. The World Café (and the world in general) was deprived of my brilliance that night, as the evening ended without my fabulous story being told. At that point I was bummed, but not defeated. Surely I'd make it next go-round!

As the years passed, I determined to try try again, this time at a Moth Story Slam at the Painted Bride Art Center. I had worked up an-other true, yet harrowing story, this one about the night our apartment neighbor threatened to kill us (yes!). Once again, I felt this tale had all the elements of a winner. I pictured myself enthralling the crowd as I described the menacing character, armed with a baseball bat, who had run up the apartment stairs cursing at us. And me nine months pregnant to boot! Obviously there was a happy ending, because I was still alive to speak, but lots of scary moments beforehand. This time, the odds were with me: a mere 21 people had put their names in, for 10 possible slots. 50-50!! I was in for sure!

I wasn't the first one chosen. No worries!! Nor was I the second. Or third. Number four was a woman whose daughter dared her to try out! She didn't even really want to do it! But that's not all! Number six was...the daughter herself! Performance lightning had struck twice in the same family!!!

Some of the remaining stories were great, some were REALLY lame. None of them, alas, was mine. The evening ended in sadness, as once more I struck out.

On the drive home, I made up my mind: no more slams for me. It's just too depressing to work hard on a piece, only to be snubbed time and again. I have no more luck there than I do winning the lottery. The mother-daughter duo especially rankled—what the heck? But after I calmed down, I took stock. I am lucky in all the ways that matter most: my incredible family, my wonderful friends, good health.

But gee, would it kill the universe to grant me one lousy shot at a story slam too?

DEFINING MOMENT?

I was in center city early yesterday afternoon, in line at Starbucks, when I checked my phone. Two missed calls from my sister C in Honolulu. A little unusual, as we try to always time our calls to one another in advance, but not unheard of. Then I got the text: *We just got alert of inbound missile. It says not a test.*

I immediately started shaking, and stepped out of line. Sheer panic set in; as I tried to call her, I blanked out on the last four digits of her phone number. By the time I reached her, she had good news: it had all been a mistake. But she described the horrific previous few minutes, trying to call all of us, possibly to say goodbye; apparently everyone in Hawaii had the same idea, because the calls weren't going through. As for me, during the few moments before I talked to her, everything else on my mind diminished in importance to nothingness. Who cared about meetings, or deadlines, or annoyances at work or home? Nothing mattered as much as my sister's survival. This dread was coupled with another: if we were indeed on the brink of nuclear war, how would any of us survive?

As we all know now, the terrifying message had been sent out in error; there was no missile heading to Oahu yesterday. But even as relief washed over me, I recognized that the message was all too credible. We are not only completely capable of the world's destruction, but powerful people with access to nuclear weapons seem to be taunting each other into action. I am aware that existence has always been fragile, but that doesn't minimize the risks and threats facing humanity right now.

Riding home on the train, I thought: how would I occupy myself if we suddenly had only a few minutes left to live? Would I fall to my knees, praying nonstop until the end? Make farewell phone calls: my children living away from me, my sister, my dearest friends? After that, would I gather my beloved Oreland family and just hold on to them? Yes! I often say that my faith, the loss of my sister Mo, and being with Mom as she passed away, have made me largely unafraid of death. But yesterday reminded me that I am still fearful. I am also saddened that life on earth may possibly not continue through Aiden and Peter's old age.

It may go out with a bang, or a whimper, or something in be-tween, but at some point life WILL end, for everyone. That point may be millions of years from now, or fifteen minutes. So may I try to live in love, the love that casts out fear. May I try to spread peace and understanding, in the hope that all of us doing so may prolong our time here.

I will never forget the sinking feeling I had in the coffee shop yesterday, but may it never define me.

BUTTERFLY EFFECT

After a cold and dreary winter (winter IS over finally, right? I'm still half-expecting another ice storm in time for Mother's Day), our much-anticipated spring is here! Daffodils and crocuses abound, and the cherry tree in our front yard is getting ready to burst into bright pink bloom. I look forward to long walks and sunshine and taking little Aiden to the playground, packing the parkas away and pulling out tee shirts and shorts. I'm so ready for warm weather that I will soon start wearing my flip flops (no matter what the thermometer reads!).

One of my favorite sights of spring is the arrival of the butterflies. Butterflies, those amazing creatures who are utterly transformed from lowly caterpillars into colorful, winged beauties, are wonderful symbols of resurrection. Their cocoons are the tombs from which they emerge into glorious new life. Butterflies remind me that death has been conquered, once and for all, and that someday we, too, will get our wings. And they remind me of something else as well...

Have you heard of the "butterfly effect"? The theory that the slightest flap of a butterfly's wings ripples on and on and impacts the weather in a far distant location at a much later date? While the flap doesn't directly cause, say, the tornado, it is one of the first conditions that set everything in motion, ending with the tornado. If the flap had not occurred, things would not have gone in the exact same direction. So even tiny things matter. They matter a lot.

The butterfly effect is an idea that reminds us that we are all connected, everything and everyone on earth, and that all of our actions have re-actions that extend far, far beyond us—for good or ill. Dropping trash on the ground matters, because too many people have done too much damage to our planet. Hurting another person matters to every person, because the harm caused diminishes us all. We are so deeply interconnected, and most often we don't even see it. So we go on acting as if what we do has no impact, when in fact the very opposite is true.

I have wondered from time to time, what difference do we really make on mission trips? After all, the team is mostly high school youth, not experienced workers. We travel to places near and far where there is great need, and spend a week trying to help. At times it feels discouraging: we will return to the Rosebud reservation this summer after 12 years away, and by all reports conditions there have not improved much, even after all this time. So what's the point of going?

I believe with all my heart that our being there does make a difference, does have an impact. Maybe some little ones who get no love at home will get a glimpse of God's love for them through our playing with them, singing with them, hugging them. Perhaps a broken door or window that lets in the bitter cold January wind can be repaired so that next winter will be more comfortable for a family living in poverty. It could be that our positive interactions will have a small part in helping to heal the deep divide between us and our Native American brothers and sisters. And just maybe our short time spent in service will be like that flap of a butterfly's wing, that will ripple on and on and affect lives far down the road, in ways we can't even imagine.

So this season, when you catch a glimpse of a Monarch or a swallowtail hovering over the flowers, remember this: Whatever we do, whatever we say, matters. It ALL matters. Because WE matter, so very much, to the One who made us all.